Drag

Drag

The Complete Story

Simon Doonan

Laurence King Publishing

What good is sitting alone in your room?
This book is dedicated to all the glamorous
eccentrics, dead and alive, who have propelled,
platformed and promoted drag over the years,
providing a destination for the destination-less,
even when it was far from easy to do so,
including, but not limited to ...

Susanne Bartsch
Chi Chi Valenti and Johnny Dynell
Gerlinde and Michael Costiff
Michou
Lee Chappell
Sister Dimension
Leigh Bowery
Mother Flawless Sabrina
April Ashley
Foo Foo Lammar
Jean Fredericks
Steve Strange
International Chrysis
Peter Gatien
Lee Brewster
Perfidia
Billy Beyond
James 'Biddie' Biddlecombe
Dorian Corey, Pepper LaBeija, Paris Dupree,
Avis Pendavis, Patricia Field and
anyone who ever hosted a voguing ball
Mother Clap
Hapi Phace
Linda Simpson
Dita Von Teese
Vaginal Davis
Adam All
Lady Bunny
and, of course, RuPaul

Author proceeds benefit
the Ali Forney Center

The Ali Forney Center houses
and protects homeless LGBTQ youth
living on the streets of New York.
Donate at www.aliforneycenter.org

CONTENTS

Introduction

I remember a time when drag seemed headed for the guillotine. The taboo was dwindling. The frisson was fizzling. What's so compelling about a man in a frock? Nada. It did not help matters that drag was becoming corporatized. No company retreat or bar mitzvah was complete without the addition of a spangled drag queen or two.

This mainstreaming of drag seemed like a death knell to many of us. In his 1996 book *The Drag Queens of New York*, Julian Fleisher noted, 'If so much of the energy of drag is generated by its outsider status, what will fuel it if it finds acceptance, even absorption, into the mainstream?' Mr Fleisher could not have foreseen the fuel that would soon start rushing down that drag inspiration pipeline. None of us could. How could we have anticipated the success of *RuPaul's Drag Race* and the new generation 'look queens' – Kim Chi, Sasha Velour, Violet Chachki and more – who are currently reinventing the notion of drag with their unprecedented and meticulous artistry. Certainly we could never have predicted the arrival of hordes of pre-teen dragsters like Lactatia and Desmond.

Kurtis Dam-Mikkelsen, aka Miss Fame, specializes in serving sickening portions of supermodel realness. In this shot, by Sanchez-Zalba, Fame pays homage to Marlene Dietrich.

The great Mathu Andersen,
drag queen, *RuPaul's Drag
Race* collaborator and makeup
artist extraordinaire, attending
World of Wonder's 1st Annual
WOWie Awards in 2013.

Acid Betty and Naomi Smalls brought their charisma, uniqueness, nerve and talent to RuPaul's DragCon LA in 2018.

And none of us foresaw the impending gender revolution. We could not possibly have guessed that by 2019 there would be more than a dozen official gender pronouns – ze, zim, sie, ey, vey, ver, tey, per, xe, etc. – and that many of these zirs and theys would be adopted by persons who would become increasingly intrigued by all aspects of drag.

We could not have known, back in the 1990s, that by the end of the second decade of the twenty-first century gender would have become so gloriously fluid, and drag so popular, that there would be heterosexual, biologically intact females – 'cisgender' to use the new terminology – who would be identifying as drag queens, and could be found waiting online at the DragCon convention in order to purchase an autographed photo of a drag queen named, for example, Sharon Needles, or simply to watch a political panel discussion about transgender rights. And who could have anticipated the vigorous politicizing and reinvigoration of drag that would be triggered by the election of Donald Trump? What is fuelling drag now? Better to ask what *isn't* fuelling drag now.

In the past, the definition of drag was simple and unqualified: whether in Shakespeare, panto or kabuki theatre, or on the bar of London's Vauxhall Tavern or the deck of a gay cruise ship, drag was defined as women's clothing worn by a man – or vice versa – for the purposes of entertainment. Trans and drag were separate. If you were a man who had transitioned, then you were no longer wearing drag, right? But now the rules have changed. In fact, there are no rules.

Cast aside your old definitions, like a pair of worn-out Louboutins. A new generation of creative souls, propelled by lightning-quick developments in social media and technology, is rewriting the drag rule book, merging genres and obliterating preconceived notions. A woman who identifies as gender-neutral and loves to drag up as a gay man? Why not? A heterosexual male artist who has a juvenile drag alter ego? Pourquoi pas? Today's dragsters are revelling in the fact that their identities are hard to pin down. My goal in this book is to introduce the uninitiated to this new wave of creative teys and pers.

'For myself, I enjoy a snug fit to better showcase my ballpark figure'. Club favourite Dina Martina has single-handedly brought back the malapropism: courtesy of Dina, Provincetown becomes 'Provence Town', a place where the biting flies are 'a perineum favourite'.

Drag queens are revolting: in 2017 a vibrant assemblage of individuals marched through the streets of Manhattan honouring Gilbert Baker (1951–2017), creator of the Rainbow Flag and co-founder of the Drag March.

I have a second, larger goal. In addition to introducing the reader to the new generation of drag proponents and activists, I also want to give these new gender warriors – and anyone else! – a bracing history lesson, a cultural history of drag, a drag history of culture, a primer encompassing everyone from Jazz Age drag king Gladys Bentley to uber-nelly French aristo Philippe, duc d'Orléans, and Japanese National Treasure Tamasaburo Bando.

My third goal, one that I share with all the drag performers of history, is to entertain. Humour is part of the DNA of drag. Long may it remain so.

NOTE: In the course of writing this book, I have done my best to use the correct pronouns and to dot all my i's and cross all my gender-identity t's. If, when reading this book, you come upon what you perceive to be a misgendering misstep, I would ask you to keep in mind the rapidly evolving nature of this new landscape, and that any flub is completely unintentional.

CHAPTER 1

Glamour Drag

A man walked into a bar. It was me, and the bar in question was a gay pub in Manchester called The Rembrandt. With little or no fanfare, a gigantic, unsmiling drag queen climbed onto a makeshift stage. Her massive red bouffant hairdo added ferocity to her predatory glamour. It was the early 1970s but she was dressed like an early 1960s hooker, in a beaded shell top, lamé miniskirt, black fishnets and slingback white stilettos (drag queens have often, wittingly or unwittingly, satirized styles from previous decades).

Suddenly the room was filled with the scratchy strains of Manuel de Falla's *Ritual Fire Dance*. Staring accusingly at the audience through ramparts of fake lashes, the drag queen produced a milk bottle containing an amber-coloured liquid. She took a huge swig, and then threw back her head. She pursed her lips and sprayed the liquid into the air like a surfacing whale. She struck a match. A cloud of fire, twice the size of her bouffant, lit up the dingy pub. I understood at that moment, my first close encounter with a drag queen, that drag is, first and foremost, a visual assault. Drag queens are not drag queens unless they can deliver some kind of retina-scorching, taboo-busting spectacle.

Violet Chachki, star of *RuPaul's Drag Race* season 7. 'With geisha-like sophistication of gesture and costume, sometimes elegant, sometimes cosmic or phantasmic, the drag queen recreates the dreamlike artifice of culture that conceals the darker mysteries of biology.' Camille Paglia

Glamour Drag

In addition to the visual assault, I was struck by the hostility underpinning this lurid tableau. This drag queen wanted not just respect, she also demanded submission. As a kid I had laughed along with Stanley Baxter and Dick Emery, beloved heterosexual icons of Brit comedy drag, but this drag queen was different. Glamorous and beautiful, she reeked of cruelty and sadism. She was, to use drag queen parlance, completely and utterly *fierce*. When I stared into the scorching gaze of this imperious fire-eating beauty, I knew I was staring at Medusa.

Sigmund Freud famously interprets Medusa's head as 'a representation of (castrated) female genitals'. The snakes in the hair also suggest male castration. In the Medusa myth, Perseus, son of Zeus, sets out to disempower the Medusa. His challenge is to get near enough to decapitate her while simultaneously avoiding her paralyzing/castrating gaze. He accomplishes this by locating the monster – female nature! – via the reflection in his shield.

Drag performs the same function as Perseus' shield. It allows us to stare down our darkest, most irrational misogynist fears, safe in the knowledge that we are looking at a parody. *That's not really a terrifying representation of the darkest mysteries of female nature. It's just your mum's hairdresser Frank wearing a frock.*

If the glamour drag queen is a Medusa symbol – a terrorizing female intent on annihilating men – small wonder that gay men, with their ambivalence about female nature, are obsessed with glamorous drag queens. Small wonder phrases like 'killing it', 'death drop' and 'slay' are part of the drag lingua franca, and small wonder that so many women take delight in the vibrant, assertive femininity of drag.

It would be a mistake, however, to think of glamour drag as being nihilistic or pointless. By confronting and satirizing our gender confusion, misogyny and castration anxieties, drag not only enthrals us, it loosens our girdles and Y-fronts, thereby mitigating our hang-ups. Drag is profoundly therapeutic.

In this chapter I will focus specifically on glamour drag queens – the Medusas. Comedy drag, glamour drag's ugly sister, will be dissected in a later chapter. As we will see, she is more Medea than Medusa. So, where did they come from, these mythic glamorous divas, these disdainful viragos, these Alaska Thunderfucks, these wickedly beautiful, domineering empresses?

Valentina, known to his Mexican parents as James Andrew Leyva, is inspired by the searing glamour of Latinx torch singers and soap-opera divas. Unsurprisingly, her name was derived from a brand of hot sauce.

Vintage drag queen magazine *Female Mimics*, from 1971.

'What is most beautiful in virile men is something feminine; what is most beautiful in feminine women is something masculine.'

SUSAN SONTAG, *Against Interpretation*, 1966

Glamour drag: an archaeology

The Victorian and Edwardian eras were noteworthy for their extreme prudishness. The sight of a piano leg might cause a lady to faint. As we will see in Comedy Drag, the music halls of the nineteenth century emphasized bawdy clowning and romping farce, thereby allowing the rabble to let off steam. Anxieties about maternal power were diffused by the sight of hideous and hilarious (straight) men lifting up their skirts to reveal frilly bloomers and knobbly knees. Then, as the twentieth century got under way, along came a cavalcade of modish glamour girls.

Like RuPaul, Julian Eltinge (1881–1941) believed in glamour and corsetry, but unlike goddess Ru, he actually bore a strong likeness to the bourgeois females in the audience. Realness and relatability were his calling cards. In a gesture that presaged the trans/drag beauty influencers of today such as Patrick Starr, Eltinge launched the *Eltinge Magazine*, dispensing beauty and fashion tips to his adoring female fans. Men, dragged up as women, teaching and beauty-splaining to women.

Francis Renault (1893–1955) was notable for his elaborate gowns and his falsetto. In 1924 he opened his own club in Atlantic City. Unlike Eltinge he would wear his costumes in the street. This generated publicity and also the occasional arrest. His fan base included a young man named Archie Leach, soon to be known as Cary Grant.

above right
Francis Renault, known as
'the Slave of Fashion'.

right
Bert Savoy, forerunner to the
sassy drag queens of today.

Mixing elegance with realness,
Julian Eltinge became drag's
first megastar. The Eltinge
Theatre in New York is named
after him.

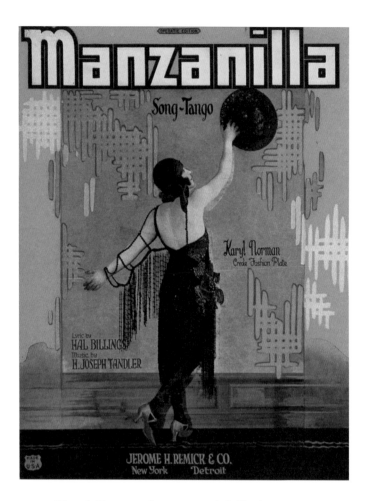

Karyl Norman (1897–1947), billed as 'The Creole Fashion Plate', was feted for his classy glamour, as well as his vocal range: he could go deep. In 1927 he starred in a Broadway musical choreographed by Busby Berkeley titled *Lady Do*. Meanwhile Bert Savoy (1876/88–1923) was a signpost to the tart-tongued drag queens of the future. His drag persona was a hip-swaying gossip – Mae West allegedly borrowed much from him – whose catchphrases included 'you slay me' and 'you don't know the half of it'. In 1916 he was making $1500 per week. He died after being struck by a lightning bolt on a Long Island beach.

Like Erté drawings come to life, these early female impersonators struck modish attitudes that emphasized supper-club style. The simple idea of a bloke undetectably lurking in an elegant frock, warbling a romantic ditty, was quite novel enough for the general public. Seduction, sadomasochism and fierceness? Those were decades away.

The hard-to-classify one-namer Barbette (1899–1973) was the first bohemian glamour drag queen. A Texas-born circus performer, Vander Clyde Broadway debuted in Paris in 1923. Here he was feted by Jean Cocteau who said of him, 'he is no mere acrobat in women's clothes, nor just a graceful daredevil, but one of the most beautiful things in the theatre. Stravinsky, Auric, poets, painters, and I myself have seen no comparable display of artistry on the stage since Nijinsky.' Later in his career Barbette was hired to teach gender illusion to Jack Lemmon and Tony Curtis for their star turns in *Some Like It Hot*.

Mr Jackie Maye and Mr Robbie
Ross backstage at the Jewel
Box Revue, a venue where
burlesque met drag. Yes, they
are men in frocks, but – stop
the presses! – these sassy
soubrettes are also alluring,
curvaceous and flirtatious.

Glamour drag starts to sizzle

The Jewel Box Revue, an all-gay troupe of 'cross-dressers', was founded in Miami in 1939 by two gay men, Doc Brenner and Danny Brown, and operated for the next three decades. The target audience was straight. The performers were billed as feminine impressionists and femme mimics. Jewel Box alumni include Lynne Carter, Ricky Renée, International Chrysis and Lavern Cummings. In addition to its sexy allure, the JBR was also noteworthy for racial diversity: in 1955 the African American future activist Stormé DeLarverie (who we will meet again in Radical Drag) was hired as MC.

By the 1950s *Playboy* magazine was on the stands and SEX was on the menu. Cultural mores were shifting rapidly. The 'permissive society' was finding its feet and shoving them into Bettie Page porno heels. Culture was getting sexier, and so was drag. The sexualization of drag was propelled by working-class gay men, living out fantasies of seducing heterosexual men and thereby becoming 'real women'.

Drag gets sexy. 'La Belle Bambi', née Jean-Pierre René, oozes seductive burlesque at a Juan-les-Pins nightclub in 1956.

Many sex workers now became drag queens, and vice versa. At this point in history, the straight drag artists took refuge in comedic drag and the gay ones began to cultivate the aggressive, sexy, diva-like personas – the Medusa! – that were the antecedents of my fire-eater and today's Drag Racers.

Balls, pageants and parades gave drag queens opportunity to preen and to hone their feminine wiles. If you could hold your own in a beauty pageant – the ultimate test of whether you could 'pass' – then how could you not be a real woman? Making a convincing impression in this milieu took an enormous amount of energy and creativity, but the drive to throw on a sash and escape the discriminatory oppression of rough inner-city life, even if only for one evening, is a powerful motivator.

Most of these balls are lost to the mists of time. One notable occasion was memorialized in a movie named *The Queen*, the denouement of which is a spectacular confrontation between Harlow, the winner, and the infinitely more deserving Crystal LaBeija.

She's about to pop off. In the movie *The Queen*, Crystal LaBeija (left) demonstrates a ferocious and commendable unwillingness to accept anything other than first place. This incendiary denouement is celebrated throughout the drag world to this day.

The 1968 *New York Times* review of *The Queen* was written by Renata Adler, a member of the American literati: 'THE QUEEN is an extraordinary documentary about the Miss All-America Camp Beauty Pageant held at Town Hall in 1967. The contestants were transvestites from all over the country – some of them winners in regional contests – judged for walking, talking, bathing suit, makeup, hairdo and, of course, beauty. The star and the winner was Harlow, a frail, blond, pouting young man, formerly Miss Philadelphia. The director was Frank Simon (his first feature film), and the movie itself is funny – not tactless – and inspired the way "The Endless Summer", of surfing, was inspired. It shows us another America.'

Vaginas for sale

In the early 1950s, Bronx-born former GI George Jorgensen became Christine, making headlines around the world by becoming a woman. Thanks to Christine Jorgensen, the concept of sex-change operations entered the public realm. Men in frocks were becoming former men in frocks. Many of the recipients went on to live happy and fulfilled lives as trans women. Some kept one sparkly stiletto parked in the drag queen milieu.

In 1958 Coccinelle underwent gender reassignment surgery, performed by pioneer Georges Burou, based in Casablanca. Dr Burou carried out many high-profile vaginoplastys, including those of acclaimed travel writer Jan Morris and socialite/restauranteuse April Ashley. Post-op, Coccinelle made headlines when she married a French journalist. She later performed frequently at the famous nightclub Le Carrousel de Paris, which also featured regular acts by other famous transsexual women like April Ashley and Marie-Pier Ysser, aka Bambi. In later life Coccinelle became a trans activist, founding an organization called Devenir Femme. Though she became a right-on trans woman, she retained the chutzpah and ferocious glamour of a drag queen.

Not every drag queen felt inclined to avail herself of the new medical advances. Danny La Rue loathed the term drag queen and preferred to be thought of as a man in a dress, starting every performance with an ice-breaking 'Watcha mates!' Like RuPaul and Lady Bunny, Danny's ability to combine comedic drag and glamour drag may well account for his astonishing success. His constant TV appearances and his legendary two-year stint at the Palace Theatre in London made him the Eltinge of the Swinging Sixties and hedonistic, liberated Seventies.

Coccinelle, originally known as Jacques-Charles Dufresnoy, was born into drag. Her mother was a flower seller at the legendary Parisian drag *boîte* Madame Arthur.

'The seduction emanating from a person of uncertain or dissimilated sex is powerful.' COLETTE

Danny La Rue worked hard to combine blokey approachability with exaggerated showgirl glamour. His signature song was 'On Mother Kelly's Doorstep', a heartwarmingly twee ditty about working-class solidarity.

Imitation: the sincerest form of misogyny?

Danny La Rue and Coccinelle were their own very individual creations. While Danny and Cocc developed their carefully crafted personas, many glamour drag queens of this period began to build reputations based on imitation. They weren't just female impersonators: they were female celeb-lookalikes and performalikes. The ability to caricature a popular icon – Shirley Bassey, Peggy Lee, Dusty et al. – was a logical next step in the evolution of glamour drag: *Not only do I resemble a woman, but I resemble a glamorous woman who you idolize.*

Charles Pierce caricatured divas like Bette Davis and Joan Crawford, who already seemed like parodies of themselves. Like Charles Busch, Danny La Rue and RuPaul, he successfully integrated comedy with glamour.

above left
So successfully did Jimmy
James impersonate Marilyn
Monroe throughout the 1980s
and '90s, that the Central
African Republic inadvertently
slapped an image of James
onto a Marilyn tribute postage
stamp.

above right
Jim Bailey studiously
avoided clownish caricature
and delivered meticulous
imitations of torch-singing
divas, whose emotional
vulnerability had special
meaning for gay audiences.
Jim Bailey's Judy lived on for
decades after the original had
withered and departed.

right
By the 1980s definitions of
glamour drag were expanding.
John Kelly debuted his
hauntingly beautiful Joni
Mitchell impersonation at
the inaugural 1985 Wigstock
festival, singing – not
lip-synching – in a Joni-
esque contralto. When Joni
eventually caught Kelly's act
she said she felt like 'Huck Finn
attending his own funeral'.
Nonetheless she gifted
Kelly her dulcimer, which he
subsequently played onstage.

MICHOU

A MONTMARTRE . DINER · SPECTACLE . TOUS LES SOIRS
80, RUE DES MARTYRS . PARIS 18 . TEL : 606.16.04

Chez Michou, the legendary
Parisian drag cabaret,
showcased brittle and
glamorous drag queens who
caricatured divas such as

Dalida, Zizi Jeanmaire and
Maria Callas. Along with
Madame Arthur, Chez Michou
was an inspiration for the
musical *La Cage aux Folles*.

By the time we got to Wigstock: the new wave

The legendary Pyramid Club in NYC's East Village was the springboard for the Wigstock festival in nearby Tompkins Square Park, and Wigstock was the catalyst for everything that followed, including Deee-Lite, Sister Dimension, Tabboo!, Lady Bunny and – drum roll! – RuPaul. This post-punk era saw an explosive growth in a new kind of drag queen culture. Suddenly drag became much hipper, smarter and, yes, postmodern. Glamour drag queens began to graze on perverse aspects of pop culture, mashing it up and spewing it back at their audience with knowing vigour. Judy and Marilyn were fine for the old gin-swilling gay audiences of the 1950s, but the Wigstock generation craved fresh sources of dragspiration. The new wave dragsters were inspired by a broad range of camp cultural offerings,

Poster for the 1995 documentary film *Wigstock: The Movie*.

Page in Linda Simpson's apartment. As drag became more stylish and less clichéd, strange and beautiful figures emerged. The 1990s saw the arrival in the East Village of the magnificent Page, John Waters's favourite drag queen, a one-namer with a cultlike following. Drag documentarian Linda Simpson remembers Page fondly: 'She was sometimes dubbed the "white Grace Jones", because of her mysterious beauty and outrageous sense of style. Despite her fierce appearance, she was a sweet and playful soul who loved being part of the wild drag scene, even though she herself was transsexual.'

including the films of John Waters and Russ Meyer, *The Sonny and Cher Show*, Mary Tyler Moore, Diana Ross (*Mahogany*), Karen Carpenter, Stevie Nicks, *Valley of the Dolls* and more. This new wave of creativity propelled drag out of the gay ghetto and into the broader culture.

Performance artists such as Leigh Bowery elevated drag out of the tacky and into the trendy. Edgy and innovative drag queens featured at super-hip clubs on both sides of the Atlantic: The Paramount, The Pyramid, The Area, Boy Bar, The Salon de Beauté, The Limelight, The Tunnel, The Blitz, The Camden Palace, Jackie 60, Kinky Gerlinky ... the list goes on.

The previously unknown Harlem voguing ball culture added gasoline to the flames. Vogue culture inspired Susanne Bartsch's groundbreaking Love Ball fundraisers, where Madonna first encountered the members of the House of Xtravaganza. No longer seen as déclassé, drag queens were welcomed – and hired! – for their ability to make an event or party seem more *au courant*. Modish drag queens like Mathu and Zaldy were seen as decorative *objets d'art*. It was only a matter of time before drag hit the runways.

Three decades before the arrival of gender-neutral runway sensation Andreja Pejić, the fashion runways were awash with drag queens such as Billy Beyond, Connie Girl (pictured here on Thierry Mugler's runway), Lypsinka and trans enigma Teri Toye.

Glamour drag à la mode

In the late 1980s the exaggerated fashion styles of the 1950s – arch, painted, bitchy and corseted à la Sophia Loren and Gina Lollobrigida – enjoyed a significant revival. The supermodels arrived and style entered a period of self-parody, setting fashion on a collision course with drag queens. The haughty remoteness of Linda, Christy and Naomi – those Medusan $10,000-a-day runway glamazons – screamed drag queen. RuPaul's hit 'Supermodel (You Better Work)' blasted on every dance floor and runway, giving us the immortal line 'Sashay! Shantay!' Models became drag queens and drag queens became models.

Starring RuPaul and shot by Albert Sanchez, this audacious ad campaign dared to use a black drag queen to market cosmetics to women.

THE ORIGINAL
M·A·C

IN HIS OWN WORDS

Supermodel Billy Erb, aka Billy Beyond, on life on the runway

'I'm from the foothills of Appalachia. It's a town of seven hundred named West Middlesex. Can you believe? Amy Sedaris and I always joke that I have lady's blood. When I looked in the mirror I always saw the face of a woman. [With his catlike eyes and delicate bone structure, Billy calls to mind a young Vivien Leigh.]

The minute I set foot in New York in the 1980s everyone – Edwige Belmore, David LaChapelle – wanted to put me in drag. I modelled from 1990 to 1994, mostly for Todd Oldham, but also for Andre Walker, BodyMap and Anna Sui. Because I looked like a girl, all I had to do was shave and show up.

Thing is, I wasn't a drag queen. I was a model impersonator. This was the era of the supermodels, and I would imitate them. The first time I was booked, I was determined not to get spooked. I went to Lee's Mardi Gras boutique [legendary trans boutique owned by Lee Brewster] and bought my gaff. When I arrived backstage I saw my friend Danilo doing the outrageous hair and Kevyn Aucoin piling on the makeup – I knew them both – and I heaved a sigh of relief. I realized all the models were in *drag*. It was all about transformation. The dressers had to work with Cindy and Veronica and this one and that one, and then me, and nobody warned them. But I never had a problem.

When I walked on to the runway my friends were standing in the back and they all howled and cheered. And in the front row Polly Mellen and Carrie Donovan and the important editors were looking around wondering what was so great about my particular outfit. After a couple of seasons the press got the picture, and then everyone started calling. Joan Rivers, Geraldo Rivera wanted to interview me, "the drag queen supermodel". But I said no. I was a model, but only on the runway or in front of a camera. I did not want them to hear my voice.

As the shows got bigger I got more serious. I would drop 5lb before the season. You have to remember that the other girls were fashion models, not fleshy, and kind of emaciated. As a boy, I could work the same look. I started to watch videos and copy the girls' tricks and gestures. Helena Barquilla! Her magnetic stare. The eyes stayed on one level, while everything else was moving. I worshipped her.

I did a double with Teri Toye [the legendary transgender model who modelled for Stephen Sprouse and Chanel in the 1980s] for a Betsey Johnson show and Teri gave me great advice. She said, "We will walk out from opposite sides. Meet in the middle, hit the pose and WAIT. And wait." The show

'Thing is, I wasn't a drag queen. I was a model impersonator.'

director was waving us on. But no. You wait. It was the hardest thing but it worked. We waited till the entire runway cleared and *then* we walked. We owned it. You would probably get fired for doing that now.

I was only a supermodel for these brief moments on the runway. Then I was back to being a boy. I never had gender dysphoria. I had to learn that particular phrase because so many people have asked me if I wanted to transition. International Chrysis would often offer me hormones.

When I look back I have no regrets. I am proud of my moves and the way I modelled. Dianne deWitt said to me, "If there's a pocket, use it." I did.'

above
Billy Beyond on the cover
of *Project X* magazine.

right
Billy (left) on Todd
Oldham's runway in 1993.

Twenty-first-century glamour drag

Back in 1999, *New Yorker* writer Holly Brubach penned *Girlfriend*, a thoughtful book on the state of drag at the end of the twentieth century. Brubach noted at the time that drag was *everywhere*. Her observations reflect a time when AIDS was becoming a less terrifying, more manageable condition, and drag, on runways and in clubs, was taking on a celebratory, exuberant, and very glamorous feel.

Brubach posited that women had, at the time, successfully retained ownership of what she calls 'the realm of appearances'. She suggests that this monopoly, by women, is a source of power that is envied by men. '[Women's] visual currency, which one hundred years ago amounted to little more than a consolation prize, has dramatically risen in value in a culture that has become increasingly visual.' She cites the supermodels – Naomi, Linda, Christy et al. – objects of desire and admiration far and wide, 'whose voices are never heard though their faces are ubiquitous'. Brubach says that such women enjoy 'the privilege of not being accountable to truth or meaning or content, of dwelling entirely on the surface'.

Brubach sees glamour drag as less of a psycho-therapeutic Medusa moment, and more an attempt, by men, to get a slice of the action. Who would not want to be worshipped simply for showing up and looking fabulous? As proof, she cites how men look and feel once they slide into a frock: 'When a man does drag today he puts on the trappings of women's power, and the naked exhilaration that ensues is so palpable, it's contagious.'

I would contend that, despite the rise of the metrosexual and the new objectification of men's bodies, despite Harvey Weinstein and #metoo, Brubach's essential point remains true. Being a woman is immensely complex and fraught with the kinds of challenges that rarely impinge upon men; however, there remains a massive privilege that attends feminine allure and beauty. All eyes are unquestioningly drawn to beauty. This is why we still worship silver-screen goddesses, and why models like Gisele are still paid

Fashion and drag in dialogue: drag has become an elaborate language which can be spoken in any context, most especially fashion. Roxanne Lowit's backstage image captures the dragtastic majesty of one of John Galliano's collections for Dior.

twenty times more than their male equivalents, why female porn stars outearn the men and why the Kardashian ladies can charge many hundreds of thousands of dollars for just one promotional Insta, while their brothers and husbands struggle to maintain a foothold. The gender pay gap is real, but the power of beauty is alive and well, and it is overwhelmingly female.

Enter the look queens

Drag evolves, drag reflects and drag shapes. Drag also seeks new ways to create a cultural frisson. As we habituate to one genre, a new, more tantalizing vision appears. As previously noted, in the past drag revelled in a truly marginalized status. It's not hard to be edgy when you are also in violation of the law. Today, in a time of broad tolerance and acceptance, drag has been challenged to find new ways

Meet Lactatia and Desmond, elfin self-identified drag queens – look queens in the making – who enlivened DragCon in 2017.

to startle and engage us. One hundred years ago the mere notion of a man in a girdle was enough to spike blood pressure. Now what? Now the look queens.

Look queens are glamour drag queens who generate shock and awe through extreme levels of cosmetic artistry. They are supermodels times a billion. They take that shimmering feminine visual realm that Brubach talked about, and magnify it for the age of Insta selfies and social media. There remains, however, a distinct whiff of the Medusa about those look queens. Fierceness is still very much in the house. With the aid of haute couture drag and never-before-seen applications of makeup, those affable young *Drag Race* contestants and others transform themselves from fresh-faced gays, barely out of their teens, into lethal goddesses, terrifying termagants, wicked queens and domineering viragos. It's not just lady power, it's lady power through paint and creativity. And politics are on the menu. As we will see in Comedy Drag and Radical Drag, this visual feminine realm is now infused with a political empowerment that puts tucking and contouring cheek by jowl with #resist and #metoo.

A visit to DragCon reveals that Medusa may have moved way beyond the previously exclusive grasp of gay males. The look queens' earnest focus on cosmetic artistry has helped to expunge any sordid and sinister overtones that linger around the word 'drag'. This change is historic and momentous. By constructing a creative, welcoming environment for cis females and young kids, RuPaul and her cast of mesmerizing divas have created a glamour drag for all.

opposite
Kim Chi gets the Sanchez-Zalba treatment. Collaborators Albert Sanchez and Pedro Zalba reverentially document the creativity of the new generation of look queens, magnifying their meticulous artistry and creating an entire new genre of art photography.

CHAPTER 2

Art Drag

When Grayson Perry first burst onto the art scene in the 1990s, many assumed his commitment to transvestism was little more than a PR ploy. Every 'Young British Artist' seemed to have some kind of gimmick, so why not drag? Over time Perry has revealed a far more complex, painful and genuine picture. In his brutally honest autobiography, *Portrait of the Artist as a Young Girl*, Perry reveals the impact of his tyrannical stepfather on the development of his obsession with drag, his kinks and his fascination with outsider artist Henry Darger. Grayson Perry has been richly rewarded for his ceramics, tapestries and paintings, his self-disclosures and his proud transvestism. In addition to winning the Turner Prize, he has also become a beloved public intellectual, up there with Mary Beard and Brian Cox.

Though Perry is the *ne plus ultra* of art drag artists, he is not the first to frock up. Drag and art work well together. The incendiary nature of drag telegraphs edgy avant-gardism and notoriety. In Butch Drag we will see how artists like Gluck and writer George Sand used drag to craft a powerful public image. Incorporating drag also enables the more experimental artists to differentiate their work from conventional artistic endeavours such as still life, landscape and portraiture.

'If a man puts on a little girl's dress he wants to be treated as a little girl and handled with care', declared Grayson Perry, the patron saint of art drag, seen here dressed as Claire, his alter ego.

Marcel Duchamp, *L.H.O.O.Q*,
1919. Duchamp performs
gender reassignment on a
sacred cow. He declared that
'Good taste is the enemy of
good art.'

The marriage of drag and art goes back to the beginning of the twentieth century, a time of mayhem and brutality. Between the fall of Baghdad, the trenches of the First World War and the bloodbath of the Russian Revolution, chaos reigned across much of the globe. As if to thumb his nose at Armageddon, Marcel Duchamp, using the pseudonym R. Mutt, submitted his now famous signed urinal to a New York art exhibition. The year was 1917. Two years later he upped the Dada by defacing a postcard of the *Mona Lisa* with a moustache and beard and calling it ART. This regendering event marked the beginning of Duchamp's drag journey, a not insignificant component of his *oeuvre*.

One year after the *Mona Lisa* debacle, Duchamp debuts his very own drag alter ego, the mysterious Rose Sélavy, a play on the French adage '*Eros, c'est la vie*' ('Eros, such is life'). Rose's low-key arrival was announced with the question 'Why not sneeze Rose Sélavy?', written on the underside of a small birdcage containing a thermometer, a cuttlefish bone and marble cubes. A year later Rose signed her name on a collage by fellow Dadaist Francis Picabia, adding a second 'r' and becoming Rrose Sélavy.

Soon after, Duchamp began dragging up and posing for photographs taken by Man Ray, fashion photographer and fellow artist. A Man Ray portrait of Rrose appeared on a perfume bottle that Duchamp labelled *Belle Haleine* ('Beautiful Breath'). Duchamp's drag dalliance, daring and incomprehensible, then and now, contributed to the artist's legend, and has had major staying power. In the intervening years Rrose has inspired everything from an oyster bar in Manhattan to a compendium of surrealist poetry.

On the heels of Duchamp we have Claude Cahun, the male alter ego of Lucy Schwob, a brave Jewish lesbian surrealist writer, photographer and trans philosopher. Cahun, who once declared that 'illusion and truth are twin children who have swapped their pink and blue ribbons', hung out with Man Ray, Salvador Dalí and André Breton, exhibiting in the surrealist show at Galerie Ratton in 1936. During the German occupation Claude and her partner and stepsister,

Duchamp photographed by Man Ray in the guise of Rrose, 1921. In 2017 a letter to *Private Eye* magazine from an Ena B. Phyllis-tyne noted the resemblance between Duchamp's drag alter ego Rrose Sélavy and Noel Fielding, co-presenter of *The Great British Bake Off*, 'who also takes the piss'. Duchamp famously admitted that he was motivated by his 'general philosophy of never taking the world too seriously – for fear of dying of boredom.'

Claude Cahun masquerades as a bodybuilder. Her photographic self-portraits make her the forerunner to artists like Cindy Sherman, Catherine Opie and Gillian Wearing.

the illustrator Suzanne Malherbe (who published books under the male pseudonym Marcel Moore), joined the Resistance and began disseminating anti-Nazi propaganda.

Cahun was eventually caught by the Germans and sentenced to death. The Allies liberated her after the War, but incarceration had damaged her health and she died in 1954, decades before her progressive ideas enjoyed wider acceptance. 'Shuffle the cards', she once said. 'Masculine? Feminine? It depends on the situation. Neuter is the only gender that always suits me.'

By the 1950s Andy Warhol was already living in New York, working as a fashion illustrator and developing the high camp sensibility that would inform his 1960s art. The archly glamorous styling in the movies and fashion mags of this era is worth noting: the cartoony eyebrows, cigarette holders, spiked heels and wasp waists of the 1950s laid down the ground rules for drag queens in decades to come, and mesmerized Warhol. According to the late

opposite
Andy Warhol, *Self-portrait in drag*, c. 1981. Transformation was exciting to Warhol. His drag alter ego was named Drella, a contraction of Dracula and Cinderella. In addition to dragging up, Andy transformed his man-self with his signature white wig, plastic surgery and corsetry.

'For a while we were casting a lot of drag queens in our movies because the real girls we knew couldn't seem to get excited about anything, and the drag queens could get excited about anything.'

ANDY WARHOL, *The Philosophy of Andy Warhol (From A to B and Back Again)*, 1975

Jack Smith's business card simply read 'exotic consultant'. Pretentious yet undeniably fabulous, performance artist, filmmaker and mouldy-glam icon Smith is best known for his movie *Flaming Creatures*, a revolutionary portrayal of transvestites, drag shows and drug orgies. He was described by John Waters as 'the only true underground filmmaker' and by Laurie Anderson as 'the godfather of performance art'.

From Warhol's 1975 series of silkscreens, cleverly titled *Ladies and Gentleman*. 'I am … fascinated by boys who spend their lives trying to be complete girls because they have to work so hard – double time – getting rid of the tell-tale male signs and drawing in all the female signs … What I'm saying is, it is very hard work.' Andy Warhol *The Philosophy of Andy Warhol (From A to B and Back Again)*, 1975

Richard Martin, one-time curator of the Met Costume Institute, 'Warhol was a blissful follower and fabricator of the pseudo-elegant'. Martin feels that 'his parvenu ignorance of good taste inspired him to a tantalizing vulgarity'.

Warhol surrendered to camp, and to drag. In the 1950s he sketched his pal Otto Fenn in drag. In the 1960s he created strange movie-star collages – Garbo's eyes, Sophia Loren's lips – producing an ersatz glamour that reeks of drag and transformation. He filmed not just his superstars, but also drag devotees and performance artists Jack Smith and Mario Montez. In the 1970s came *Ladies and Gentlemen*, a series of artworks depicting black and Hispanic drag queens in New York City, including trans icon Marsha P. Johnson.

opposite
Beginning in the 1970s, artist and jewellery-maker Andrew Logan staged his Alternative Miss World contests in London in improbable locations. Mostly male contestants – gay directors Derek Jarman and John Maybury both gave it a whirl – opted for names like Miss Holland Park Walk and Miss Carriage. Host Andrew oversaw the bacchanalian proceedings wearing his signature demi-drag frock by Zandra Rhodes.

right
Mime artist Lindsay Kemp brought drag and sophisticated decadence into the pop milieu. He was best known for his onstage collaborations with David Bowie during the glam-rock era.

During the 1970s, economic recessions on both sides of the Atlantic depressed the art market. With their work less exalted, many artists felt liberated and a new fluidity arose between the worlds of art, fashion and music. Warhol became a Studio 54 night owl, hanging out with fashion designers, celebs and models. New York drag clubs like The Gilded Grape became trendy gathering places, and artists found spontaneous outlets for their art drag impulses, bringing their creativity to the wider cultural landscape.

The post-punk era was, in many ways, more interesting than punk itself. There was an unleashing of creativity in music, fashion and art. A blizzard of new faces, mags and ideas rained down, including Judy Blame, *The Face*, the New Romantics, John Galliano, the Pyramid Club, BodyMap, *ID* magazine, The Blitz, Susanne Bartsch, Keith Haring, Jean-Michel Basquiat, Stephen Sprouse, Charles Atlas, trans doll-maker/artist Greer Lankton and trans model Teri Toye. These key figures were not the children of the famous. They were (mostly) working-class kids from the sticks who, propelled by new and original ways of seeing the world, had clawed their way out of obscurity into the underbelly of the big city. They had something to say.

In 1993 Leigh Bowery, pictured here with his wife and collaborator Nicola Bateman, told *The Sunday Times* of London, 'Things that used to embarrass me, like nudity and gender confusion, don't any more. I have used my discomfort to explore these areas.' He told *HQ* mag that what interested him was 'the idea that something can be frightening and heroic and pathetic all at the same time'.

opposite
When artist Steven Cohen was arrested in 2014, having tied a live rooster to his penis in a Parisian tourist spot in front of (among others) a group of nuns, I swear I could hear Leigh Bowery chuckling words of encouragement from on high.

right
EVA & ADELE claim to have come from the future in a time machine, landing after the fall of the Berlin Wall in 1989. Since then, with their bald heads, futuristic makeup and matching costumes, they have become global art-world royalty. Unlike Leigh Bowery, their entire waking lives – shopping, eating and visits to the dentist – are lived as a public art performance. Their motto is 'wherever we are is a museum'. EVA (male) & ADELE (female) waited until German law allowed them to marry as two women. They smile continually. If they don't feel like smiling they don't go out.

In 1981 a young lad named Leigh Bowery moved to London from Sunshine, a suburb of Melbourne. This was the beginning of an astonishing art drag journey that would reach unimaginable levels of artistic originality, perversity and creativity. Saftig Leigh's anarchic brand of self-presentation incorporated drag but exploded past any existing definitions, beyond performance art and into madness. Bowery collaborator and biographer Sue Tilley recalls him saying, 'If I have to ask, "Is this idea too sick?", I know I'm on the right track.'

The excesses of the performances are legendary: Leigh evacuating his bowels on the stage at the annual Wigstock dragfest in NYC; Leigh 'giving birth' to wife Nicola; Leigh piercing his cheeks with catgut and safety pins to achieve a more *Vogue*-y expression; Leigh turning himself into a busty 'woman' with brutal duct-taping and tucking; Leigh the living sculpture installed at the Anthony d'Offay Gallery in Mayfair; and Leigh, the artist's muse, posing naked and massive for painter Lucian Freud. Leigh died of AIDS in 1994 and is greatly missed. His influence lives on in the realms of makeup, fashion and drag performance.

Strike a pose: the art of drag photography

In 1966 Diane Arbus shot a career-making image. Titled *A Young Man in Curlers at Home on West 20th Street*, this photograph became iconic and spawns brilliant amateur recreations to this day. Since *Young Man in Curlers,* drag queens and trans folk have been captured by artist–photographers with increasing enthusiasm. The reasons for this are obvious. The edgy contradictions that make a compelling photograph are ever-present in drag and trans. Drag magnifies issues of race, class and gender. Drag makes good art.

opposite
In the late 1950s, Swedish art photographer Christer Strömholm lived with the transvestites and transsexuals of the Place Blanche in Paris. The resulting images combine the edgy chic of Avedon with the bleak urban reportage photography of William Klein or Vivian Maier.

above
Art photographer Henny Garfunkel reassigned Brooke Shields's gender, and class, for a 1990 *Paper* magazine cover shoot. The headline? 'Pretty Butch'.

David LaChapelle, *My Own Marilyn*, 2002. David LaChapelle does Warhol doing Amanda Lepore doing Marilyn. LaChapelle and muse Lepore have enjoyed a fertile and long-standing artistic collaboration.

Art drag for everyone

Marcel Duchamp's early forays into art drag now seem quite genteel. Today's art drag scene is, by comparison, quite explosive, reflecting the new gender/diversity politics that have developed so fascinatingly in recent years. Artists are not only deconstructing preconceived notions of male and female, but they have also blurred the lines between art drag and drag queen/look queen drag.

Emblematic of the new politically charged state of art drag is Victoria Sin, a cisgender non-binary female who goes by the pronoun 'they' and performs/presents as a drag queen. Victoria takes the exaggerations of established drag queens like Lady Bunny and places them in the context of politics and art, declaring, 'It is defiance to have femininity exalt me as it should.'

Victoria Sin's wiggy wigs, fake bust and cartoony maquillage allow them to parody and explore aspects of femininity and power.

Another rising star is Johannes Jaruraak, a 26-year-old Berliner who performs using the name Hungry. Johannes goes by he. Hungry goes by she. In 2017 *The New York Times* described Hungry's act: 'The performance bore no sign of drag's defining camp. It was sombre, with no touch of melodrama. But it was undeniably drag: weird and apocalyptic, drag as seen through a cracked mirror.'

Narcissister, the brave new face of conceptual art drag, appears to be constructed from a random collection of window-display props and mannequin parts. The child of Moroccan and African American parents, Narcissister uses performance art to focus on race, gender and sexuality. A recent show of disturbing self-portraits displays the artist, looking somewhat mangled, wearing fake boobs and a selection of masks and wigs. Her *pièce de résistance* is a 'reverse

Young drag performers such as Berlin's Hungry now combine the surrealism and anarchy of Leigh Bowery with the cosmetic finesse of the look queens of *RuPaul's Drag Race*.

striptease'. During this avant-porn performance she begins naked and
dresses herself in clothing extracted from her various body cavities.

The dynamism of the current art drag performance scene
is propelling the art world forward. The *enfants terribles* of the
1990s and 2000s, such as Damien Hirst and Tracey Emin, seem
by comparison almost conventional. While today's performance
dragsters find new and decorative ways to be appalling and
provocative, they simultaneously – wittingly or unwittingly –
pay homage to their forebears. There is a delightful whiff of Cahun
and Duchamp in the work of Hungry, Cohen and Narcissister.

CHAPTER 3

Butch Drag

'Women get treated bad. They get beat. They get robbed. They get dogged', declared drag queen Pepper LaBeija, back in the 1980s. The legendary Mother of the House of LaBeija was explaining why she had never undergone gender reassignment surgery. Pepper's dark observations about the perils and disadvantages of womanhood provide a meaningful context for butch drag. If being a woman is so fraught with challenges, small wonder that so many, throughout history, have found reasons to defrock, drag up and man up.

The new face of the drag kingdom: Adam All, aka Jen Powell, hosts a monthly drag king club night in London named Boi Box. Adam's chosen male genre is best described as Technicolor metrosexual geek chic.

In *The Drag King Book*, Judith 'Jack' Halberstam writes that, 'there is a considerable difference between those women who cross-dress for fun and maintain a stable relation to femininity, and those kings whose performances and costumes are part of their lives as gender-ambiguous people.' As a cis male I would not dream of disputing this assertion: I would, however, suggest that there are certain broad overlapping motivations that unite drag kings, trans men and those who get a kick out of occasionally dressing up like Elvis.

Butch Drag

Power

The twentieth century saw the emancipation of women and a masculinizing of female attire. Two World Wars played a role: tailored butch uniforms embolden the wearer and inspire respect in others. Women began to demand the same rights enjoyed by their male siblings and colleagues. A growing number of women started to escape the bondage of domesticity and to mingle with men in factories and schools. The hothoused, corseted Victorian ideal of womanhood began to wither, in its place a new generation of power dykes.

Poor women had fewer choices, whereas wealthy upscale butches were better positioned to take advantage of this first feminist wave. Many iconic twentieth-century dragsters were women of privilege. They had the 'fuck you' money that allowed them to lead lives of rule-breaking independence, mirroring their powerful brothers and fathers. They also had the wherewithal to head for Savile Row and indulge in extensive orgies of custom tailoring.

opposite
Rockabilly style, with its heady mix of strutting, Elvis-inspired masculinity and feminine mascara-wearing vulnerability is a perennial drag king favourite.

right
These two natty power dressers are expressing the inexpressible. In the sexually anxious nineteenth-century society, euphemisms abounded, and 'trousers' were referred to as 'inexpressibles'.

Lady Una Troubridge and writer Radclyffe Hall, author of the famous – and famously depressing – lesbian novel *The Well of Loneliness*, were one of the great power couples of herstory, up there with Gertrude Stein and Alice B. Toklas. Their lives throbbed with sartorial gender fluidity: in the early 1920s Troubridge (seated) adopted a tailored look similar to Hall's mannish drag. Later she reverted to more femme styles, as pictured. After Hall died, Troubridge went back to butch drag: her tailor recut Hall's suits for Lady Una, which seems like a fitting way to memorialize her deceased butch.

Among Joe Carstairs's many idiosyncrasies was her longtime devotion to a small doll – clearly for Joe, the only acceptable male companion was small, inert, free of genitalia and stuffed with kapok – which she named Lord Tod Wadley. His Lordship was cremated alongside his mistress.

above

The artist Gluck, born Hannah Gluckstein (1895–1978), was a rule-breaking one-namer from a creative Jewish family. Her paintings were striking and modern, as were her natty suits. Mannish attire – eccentric, bold, provocative – made Gluck memorable and gave her entry into the world of aristo-bohemia. She had a fling with celebrity florist Constance Spry.

Standard Oil heiress Joe Carstairs, born in 1900, refused to sit back and passively envy the physical and sexual freedom enjoyed by the powerful dudes in her milieu. The speedboat addict and lifelong dandy led a life of adventure and swagger – and drag. According to her biographer, Kate Summerscale, 'Joe would walk into a room, head straight for the mirror and strike a pose, three fingers inside her jacket pocket, the thumb and little finger outside. "Marvellous", she exclaimed.'

'Instead of being an angry woman, I became a funny man.'

MO B. DICK

Butch drag did not loom large during the second feminist wave. The hippies and counter-culture 'wombyn' of the 1960s and 1970s were anxious to distance themselves from anything that might be construed as celebrating patriarchal masculinity. Fast forward to the 1990s. Irony rules. Butching it up, aping the style of men and making it their own, has put many women in the driver's seat and improved their lives. While aristocratic butches like Hall and Carstairs adopted the styles of the powerful (male) landed gentry, the drag kings of the 1990s, being largely working class, gravitated to macho stereotypes such as Teddy boys, cholos, mafiosi and greasers. They satirized the excesses of macho men while enjoying the benefits of butch privilege. Mo B. Dick, an icon of this era, tells it like it was: 'Creating a rough and tough rebellious rockabilly drag king character allowed me to say and do whatever the hell I wanted. I had a blast being loud, crass and cheesy and the audience loved it. It was incredibly refreshing to walk the streets of NYC in men's shoes and not be catcalled or harassed. Now I got to do the catcalling.'

above
In early 1996, a drag king named Mo B. Dick started Club Casanova in New York City. It was the world's first weekly club night to showcase drag kings. The cavalcade of featured talent included Dred, Justin Kase, Shon, Labio, Lizerace, Antonio Caputo, Sir Real, Murray Hill, and Mo himself.

Style

The desire to appear sharp and cool was a significant motivator to the drag kings of yore, nowhere more so than in gay Paree. The libertine ethos of nineteenth-century Paris encouraged all kinds of glamorous perversions and inversions, including the wearing of deliciously stylish drag. Amantine Lucile Aurore Dupin, aka George Sand, lived the life of Riley (or the French equivalent). She had an affair with Chopin, she hung out with Flaubert, Liszt and Balzac, she smoked tobacco in public and, most importantly, she wore chic, masculine men's clothing. Her exquisite brand of French couture drag made her noteworthy and memorable and helped her craft the George Sand brand.

The French were in the butch drag vanguard. Toulouse-Lautrec was painting dykes in severe costumes while British artists were still churning out earnest landscapes and dreary aristocratic portraits. French authors were writing about butch lesbian hangouts, while the likes of Wordsworth, Thomas Hardy or Henry James would never have entertained such an appalling idea. In Emile Zola's 1880 novel *Nana*, the eponymous anti-heroine discovers Laure's, a lesbian restaurant on the rue des Martyrs. In this decadent spot, up-for-anything Nana takes note of a cheeky young man as he unleashes his charms on a table of vastly fat women. Only when the person in question laughs, revealing a swelling bosom, does Nana realize that she is observing a dandified butch in bloke's clothing.

An early cover design for the infamous 1920s novel *La garçonne* ('Bachelor Girl'). The risqué storyline concerns Monique, an audacious mademoiselle who dresses like a man, smokes cigarettes and has multiple sexual partners of both sexes.

A new generation of girls – playing sports, smoking, drinking and refusing to be corseted – embraced simpler, more masculine styles of dress, invented and promoted by designers such as Coco Chanel and Madeleine Vionnet. Butch drag has never been more chic.

The post-War era was a time when women, especially American women, reverted to hyper-femininity, epitomized by movie stars like Marilyn, Liz, Sandra Dee and Doris Day. Corsets made a comeback. This period marked the lull between first- and second-wave feminism. The gender binary ruled. Domesticity was fetishized. Perfectly coiffed Stepford Wives scurried around their kitchens wearing ruffled organdy aprons over their pastel sweater sets. It took a Frenchman to save the world from the folly of these regressions.

Yves Saint Laurent put women in drag and started a revolution. 'Chanel freed women. I empowered them', he said. But there was more to it than empowerment: YSL understood the truth about butch drag.

Knee-deep in style in 1930s Paris, flappers and garçonnes get acquainted at Le Monocle, a legendary Parisian lesbian club. *We might be marginal, but you have to admit we look fabuleux!*

The French call it *le chien* (the dog). When a woman has *le chien*, she has a certain edgy, haughty, stylish, intelligent allure, like a fox. When Merle Oberon played French literary drag king George Sand in the movie *A Song to Remember*, she exuded *le chien* from every seam.

On the right chick, a butch suit can actually emphasize femininity. While a tough butch dyke may achieve greater levels of butchness by donning a suit and tie, the same cannot be said for a more feminine type of girl. The suit has the reverse effect. Fragility and femininity are underscored and magnified. (The reverse process happens with burly hairy men. A girly dress on a very blokey bloke will amplify the masculine traits.)

The YSL suit was adopted by stylish, influential women. In the 1970s it filtered down to the mainstream, and the workplace, where hordes of newly recruited women were anxious to appear competent and to repel unwanted sexual invitations. Pantsuits banished the ditsy ruffled femininity of the previous generation and became ubiquitous.

Money

Feeling powerful and looking stylish are significant motivators. But, for most women, the desire to achieve financial independence is prime. Earning a living, making a buck – every girl needs a job.

Within the world of entertainment, men in drag are undeniably more common than women in drag. It would, however, be a mistake to come away with the impression that women in drag were missing from the historical landscape of entertainment drag. Not every gal was inclined to join, or appropriately shaped for, the chorus line. How to stand out? Buy a suit and release your inner butch.

Aged 16, Gladys Bentley moved to New York City from Philadelphia. Before long she had recorded eight tracks, and received a $400 cheque (equivalent to $5,500 today). A gay speakeasy needed a male pianist. Eyes-on-the-prize Gladys dragged up – slicked-back hair, top hats, short tux jackets, white dress shirts and bow ties – and tickled the ivories in front of a chorus of drag queens. Soon she was earning $125 per week. Next stop the Ubangi Club on Park Avenue. It was the art deco 1930s, and soon Gladys was bringing home enough bacon to rent an apartment nearby, with servants and a swanky automobile.

After the 1933 repeal of prohibition, the Harlem speakeasies declined and Gladys relocated to southern California, where she repackaged herself as 'America's Greatest Sepia Piano Player' and the 'Brown Bomber of Sophisticated Songs'. When the McCarthy era arrived, Gladys was harassed for wearing men's clothing. She switched back to frocks, married a dude, and took hormones to cure her gay thing. She documented her journey in an article for *Ebony* magazine entitled 'I Am a Woman Again'. She died of pneumonia at the dawn of the 1960s, aged 52.

Gladys Bentley (1907–60), blues singer, pianist, entertainer and gender revolutionary, was a pillar of the 1920s Harlem Renaissance. In a passage from his autobiography *The Big Sea*, poet Langston Hughes described her as 'a large, dark, masculine lady, whose feet pounded the floor while her fingers pounded the keyboard – a perfect piece of African sculpture, animated by her own rhythm'.

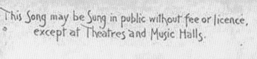

Box 13

The Latest Chap on Earth.

CHORUS.

He has the latest thing in collars, the latest thing in ties,
The very latest specimen of girly girls, with the latest blue blue eye,
He knows the latest bit of scandal, in fact he gave it birth,
But when it comes to getting up of mornings hes the latest chap on earth.

WRITTEN AND COMPOSED BY

E. W. ROGERS,

Sung by

MISS VESTA TILLEY,

Copyright.

Price 4/=

LONDON:
FRANCIS, DAY & HUNTER, 142 CHARING CROSS ROAD,
(OXFORD STREET END,)
Publishers of Smallwood's Celebrated Pianoforte Tutor, Smallwood's 55 Melodious Exercises, Etc.
NEW YORK: T. B. HARMS & Cº. 18 EAST 22ⁿᵈ STREET.
Copyright MDCCCXCIX in the United States of America, by Francis, Day & Hunter.

H. G. BANKS, Lith.

Telegraphic Address:
ARPEGGIO LONDON.

Bentley was a one-off. In the Harlem heyday, brave and bawdy Gladys would sing in a deep sexy growl while flirting with female audience members. As James Wilson writes in *Bulldaggers, Pansies, and Chocolate Babies*, 'she exerted a "black female masculinity" that troubled the distinctions between black and white and masculine and feminine'. Though Gladys was utterly unique, she came out of the cheeky ribald music hall tradition where male impersonation enjoyed enormous popularity.

The gigantic acclaim of a male impersonator like Vesta Tilley is hard for us to understand. It's worth remembering that women were often forbidden, by custom and law, from wearing male attire. The taboo factor was vastly higher than it is today. Tilley worked hard to vanquish any hint of vice or sleaze from her public image. She made a point of wearing sumptuous high-fashion frocks offstage, thereby maintaining an image of heterosexual opulence and respectability. Her husband, Walter de Frece, was knighted in 1919 for his services in World War I. As a result, Tilley became Lady de Frece.

opposite
Matilda Alice Powles (1864–1952) adopted the stage name Vesta Tilley at the age of 11, and went on to become a star on both sides of the Atlantic for over 30 years.

Ella Wesner (1841–1917) learned the craft of male impersonation while serving as dresser to the legendary Annie Hindle. Both women successfully introduced British music hall material to vaudeville audiences, and both women generated sizzling headlines after embarking on daring same-sex elopements.

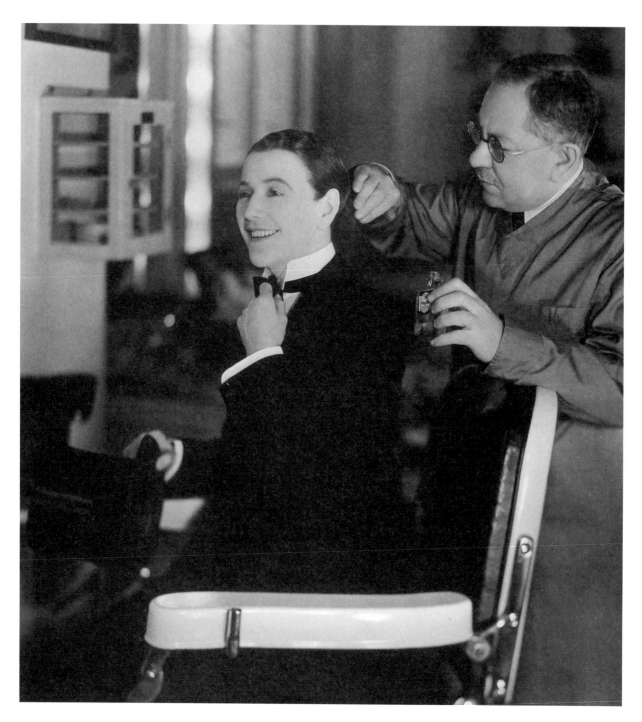

American-born Ella Shields (1879–1952), pictured here with cosmetics icon Max Factor, was a big hit in the UK, most notably with her parody of a Vesta Tilley song titled 'Burlington Bertie from Bow'. Shields's version, written by her husband/manager William Hargreaves, cleverly depicted Bertie as a moth-eaten hobo with delusions of grandeur: 'I'm Burlington Bertie, I rise at ten thirty / And saunter along like a toff / I walk down the Strand with my gloves on my hand / Then I walk down again with them off.'

Hetty King (1883–1972) was a hugely popular male impersonator in Victorian music halls, performing for over 70 years. When she opened on New York's Broadway, she was billed as 'England's greatest star'. She popularized the song 'All the Nice Girls Love a Sailor' (aka 'Ship Ahoy!'). This ditty was riddled with subtle double entendres for any gays, male or female, in the audience. Hetty was married twice, both times to men. As with Tilley, butch drag afforded her status and vast amounts of money.

As Tilley and the other famous male impersonators of yesteryear demonstrate, dragging up was lucrative. Audiences paid good money to watch cheeky women lampoon the men in the audience. This golden age of butch drag did not last forever. Male impersonation eventually lost its mainstream novelty value. Today's entertainment stars still use drag, but judiciously, knowing that it has to authentically reflect some genuine aspect of their identity.

Fey is the new butch

Butch drag has given women power, style and money. The drag king pioneers made careers out of satirizing masculine advantage, thereby gaining a modicum of emancipation for themselves. Today things are changing. Many young people reject the gender binary, so dressing with heavy-handed masculinity, aping the patriarchy in the era of the Harvey Weinstein harassment saga, does not sit well with them. Today the goals of butch drag seem more idealistic and are connected to self-expression and identity. Drag gave solidarity to lesbians in the past. It now performs the same function to the burgeoning transgender movement.

A growing cohort of women and trans men are taking the butch out of butch drag. Stephen Ira, the trans son of Annette Bening and Warren Beatty, cited Truman Capote – the gay writer known

k.d. lang
drag

The 1980s and 1990s was a great time for riot grrrls and dyke power. Enter k.d. lang, the statuesque butch with the voice of an angel. Whether serving lounge lizard or rockabilly dandy, angular k.d. cut a dashing romantic figure. This image was shot by Albert Sanchez for her 1997 album titled *Drag*. Now, with a shelf full of Grammies and a global fan base, activist lang is probably the most successful and talented drag king of all time. However, her clothing does not register as drag, because it is more about self-expression, a genuine reflection of the wearer.

'I don't believe in men's wear or women's wear. I just like what I like', says singer and actress Janelle Monáe, whose retro garçonne style made her a radical standout from the porno chic and obsessive focus on curvaceous 'hotness' that dominated the 2000s.

for his floaty foulards and floppy chapeaux – as a style inspiration. Dan Savage, the legendary sex-advice podcaster and politico, now receives calls from biologically intact females – with gender-neutral pronouns – who identify as gay males. Adam All, the club maestro responsible for London's Boi Box, dresses like a fey Justin Bieber. In an era when old-school masculinity is seen as toxic, it makes perfect sense that trans men and drag kings are seeking new archetypes Concerns about power, style and money – survival! – have been replaced by a freewheeling desire to develop a nuanced, fluid identity. Clearly, in the coming years, the definitions of drag must expand to include women who identify as non-macho males and present accordingly.

CHAPTER 4

Black Drag

A vis Pendavis, Kennedy Davenport, Jasmine Masters, Angie Xtravaganza, Mona Foot, Nina Bo'Nina Brown, Connie Girl, The Vixen, Chi Chi DeVayne, Peppermint ... these are a few of my favourite black drag queens. Whether finger popping, reading, mopping, gagging, voguing, talking to the hand, werking, twerking, throwing shade, serving genius and overness, being legendary, or simply giving realness, the black drag queen is an enduring icon of fascination and inspiration. She generously and magnanimously enriches the culture, often receiving comparatively little in return, and we must all bow down before her. #gratitude.

The Medusan ferocity that characterizes glamour drag queens is amplified in the black drag queen, and augmented with unique black irony and wit. The black drag queen is both comedic and glamorous. The black drag queen is fierce. This fierceness is not a new thing. In *Portrait of Jason*, a noteworthy 1960s documentary about a genial black hustler directed by Shirley Clarke, we already encounter the full circle snap, the high five of the black drag queen. While he waits for his dope dealer, charming Jason, who with his trendy round glasses resembles a young, black David Hockney – spins

The positive impact of RuPaul on drag and on the broader culture is immeasurable. *Can I get an Amen up in here?* Photo by Albert Sanchez.

On 27 July 1969, one month after Stonewall, courageous and stylish individuals gathered in New York's Washington Square Park to support gay rights. This event, initially dubbed Gay Liberation Day, was repeated the following year, and eventually became Gay Pride Day.

yarns from his chequered past. One anecdote concerns two drag queens befriended while Jason was incarcerated in Rikers Island. He subsequently bumps into them on New York's 14th Street, where they are holding court after a shoplifting expedition. Jason describes in hilarious detail how, every so often, one or other of the drag queens would windmill her arm through the air and snap her fingers. A passing cop imitates the gestures and asks, 'Why are you ladies always doing this?' One drag queen (called Kitty Kunt) executes yet another massive circle followed by a zigzagging finger snap, and replies, 'Honey, I'll never tell' (with another circle snap). Such is the mysterious, all-knowing charisma of the black drag queen.

Citizens with marginal status have always contributed disproportionately to the culture. Jews, with their Yiddish, gave us chutzpah, schlepping, schmatta, kvetching. And so it is with black drag, only more so. Black drag goes way beyond a list of words. That fierce attitude has not only come to define contemporary drag, but has also infected pop culture and fashion and style. It is the great gift of the black drag queen.

Why is black drag such a rich source? If creativity and originality is a function of marginal status, then the black drag queen wins the jackpot. Jason was marginalized by his blackness and gayness, but Kitty Kunt was black, gay, trans and homeless. She was marginalized from society, the gay community and her own community. To be black, gay and *en travesti*? Kitty Kunt and her sisters hit the marginal motherlode.

opposite
BeBe Zahara Benet, winner of *RuPaul's Drag Race* season 1, serving leonine fierceness. Photo by Albert Sanchez.

The black drag Hall of Fame

Hall of Famers like Pansy Club compère Karyl Norman and Gladys Bentley, mega-butch symbol of the Harlem Renaissance, have already erupted in other parts of this book, and we will meet trans activist martyr Marsha P. Johnson in Radical Drag. There are, however, so many more notable individuals of colour, some more famous than others. All of them have that mystical creative charisma that attends the black drag queen.

Jackie Shane: soul sister

Jackie Shane's poignant story reflects the discriminatory attitudes of life in the Jim Crow South, where, from the age of 13, she identified as a woman in a man's body. In the late 1950s she immigrated to the more tolerant city of Toronto. Wearing wigs and sequined silk frocks she performed soulful sets to nightclub audiences.

Though her personal style was remarkably chic and sophisticated, Jackie was a cool cat. She hung out with Jimi Hendrix and performed alongside Etta James, Jackie Wilson and The Impressions. Her one hit, 'Any Other Way', is filled with subtle communications to the gays and trans folk in her audience. In 1971 she moved back to Nashville and embraced a premature Garbo-esque retirement. 'I was just being me', she told *The New York Times* in 2016. 'I never tried to explain myself to anyone – they never explained themselves to me.'

In 2017 an anthology of recordings was released. When asked about performing again for her not insignificant cult fan base, Jackie responded, 'I'm going to have to school these people again.'

Pepper LaBeija (top centre): giving the Egyptian effect

The old drag pageants of Harlem and elsewhere, with their showgirl costumes of feathers and sequins, began to lose lustre in the 1970s. Suddenly there was a new upstart in town: f-a-s-h-i-o-n. As black models like Naomi Sims, Pat Cleveland, Iman and Beverly Johnson gained prominence, a rabid fashion fixation gripped the younger black queens, eclipsing the showgirl drag aesthetic that was front and centre in the movie *The Queen*. The Ebony Fashion Fair, a touring promotional runway show sponsored by *Ebony* magazine, fuelled the fire. Poses from *Vogue* began to find their way on to the dance floors of gay black nightlife, at nightclubs like the Paradise Garage in downtown Manhattan and Catch One in Los Angeles.

The increasing cultural obsession with fashion, shoulder pads, and the kind of sartorial richesse exhibited on shows like *Dynasty* and *Dallas* had seismic impact, especially on communities excluded from posh society. These new style-obsessed queens responded by forming fashion gangs or 'houses'. 'Crossover was beginning in earnest in 1983, when Mother Kevin Omni threw the first House of Omni Ball ... The House of Omni Ball also marked the debut of the House of Xtravaganza, and like it or not, the balls have never been the same since', writes Chi Chi Valenti, voguing historian, in the catalogue for Susanne Bartsch's 1989 Love Ball, an AIDS fundraiser inspired by the ball culture. In the same essay, Valenti identifies no fewer than 42 recognized houses. The names reveal the new obsession with *la mode*: Adonis, Afrika, Bancroft, Cameo, Chanel, Christian, Corey, Danka, Del Rios Magnifique, Diamonds, Dior, Dontierre, Dupree, Ebony, Echelons, Elegant, Elite, Field,

Grace, Grandeur, Jandell, LaBeija, Lakins, La May, La Wong, Legend, Lloyd, Magnifique, Mahogany, Marquese, Montana, Ninja, Omni, Overness, Pendavis, Plenty, Princess, St. Laurent, Unique, Votique and Xtravaganza.

Pepper LaBeija's official title was Mother of the House of LaBeija. Founded in 1970 by Crystal LaBeija (she of the legendary smackdown in the documentary *The Queen*), the House of LaBeija epitomized the ferocious pride that was needed to become legendary. Pepper underscores the dominance of LaBeija (pronounced la-BAY-zha) with one simple sentence: 'The whole of New York is wrapped up in being LaBeija.'

The miracle of Pepper is that she transitioned from the world of pageants to the new stylish ball culture, bringing her feathers and costumes with her. Pepper's haughty Egyptoid performances – she would sand dance back and forth in profile like Nefertiti come to life – and,

most importantly, her waspish musings were immortalized in the cult movie *Paris Is Burning*, the mind-blowing, life-changing, chakra-opening, landmark 1990 documentary that unleashed the world of voguing onto the culture.

I refer to Pepper as 'her' simply because I feel that, genitalia aside, this is what she would have wanted. 'I never wanted to have a sex change', intones the well-moisturized Pepper as she is filmed dragging on a ciggie in her flatteringly lit apartment. 'Having a vagina doesn't mean you're gonna have the fabulous life.'

Pepper LaBeija went to the great runway in the sky on 14 May 2003, between Mother's Day and Father's Day. The timing is entirely appropriate, since Pepper LaBeija was both a mother and a father: her *New York Times* obituary revealed the startling fact that 53-year-old Pepper had left behind two children, a son and a daughter.

Dorian Corey: showgirl sage

During *Paris Is Burning*, we are treated to the intimate spectacle of Dorian Corey, the Mother of the House of Corey, a linebacker-sized trans woman, applying her maquillage while reminiscing about her life and dispensing heavy philosophical drag queen wisdom. Director Jennie Livingston cleverly deploys the 6'2" Dorian to unravel the mores and terminology of the codified Harlem ball culture, for instance to explain the concept of 'throwing shade': 'Shade is: "I don't tell you you're ugly but I don't have to tell you because you know you're ugly", and that's shade.'

Not only was Dorian Corey an articulate sage, she was also a fearless vigilante, as evidenced by the fact that she shot and killed an intruder and successfully hid his body in a plaid garment bag for over 25 years – a story that rocked the drag world

and became a *New York* magazine cover story. When Livingston filmed La Corey in the shabby glitz of her West 140th Street apartment, she had no idea that, a few feet away, a body with a gunshot wound to the head was decomposing inside the closet. The partially mummified body was only discovered when, in 1993, 56-year-old Dorian sadly succumbed to AIDS. Reluctant though one is to condone violence of any kind, it is hard, especially given the unparalleled levels of brutality directed at trans and drag – and the fact that the corpse in question was that of a convicted rapist and robber – to see Dorian as a cold-blooded killer.

What gave Dorian her homicidal carte blanche? Scrappy Dorian's life reads like the screenplay for a film-noir Lana Turner movie: she escaped rural hell and snagged a window-dressing gig in a Buffalo department store. In the 1950s she came to New York and studied art at Parsons. The lure of the sequin propelled her into showbusiness and a starring role in the legendary Pearl Box Revue. Dorian became an integral part of this tinselled troupe. Her speciality? Dorian had a unique talent for striking glamorous and artistic attitudes while clutching a live boa constrictor.

Time was not particularly kind to Dorian Corey. Her showbiz dreams culminated in a lip-synching gig at Sally's Hideaway (the tawdry but fun 1990s trendy trans hangout located opposite the old *New York Times* offices). It was in the underground world of the Harlem voguing balls that she had shone brightest. Here, Dorian Corey was no spangled has-been: she was the well-respected, dignified Mother of the House of Corey, guiding and chiding her 'children' as they competed to win the coveted ball trophies. In *Paris Is Burning* Dorian, like rivals Pepper LaBeija, Avis Pendavis, Paris Dupree and Angie Xtravaganza, reveals herself to be a forceful, wise, beneficent beatch with real leadership skills. One comes away asking the question, 'How fierce and fabulous would America be if it was ruled by black drag queens?'

Vaginal Davis: queen of kunst

Conceptual artist, cultural provocateur, proponent of 'terrorist drag', self-described 'sexual repulsive' and now international art-world treasure, Vaginal Davis made her name on the LA club punk/performance scene of the 1980s and 1990s. No medium is alien to her: videos, paintings (created using cosmetics), xeroxed zines, the DJ booth, installations, punk-rock performances. Dominic Johnson writes in _Frieze_ magazine, 'She critiques both the gallery system and the larger cultural trend that it mirrors, with tongue-in-cheek self-exploitation and rude provocations of racial and gender confusion.'

'My late great mother Mary Magdelene Duplantier looked very much like Lena Horne with her black Creole colouring from her father and high cheekbones from her Choctaw Indian mother, who had grown up on a reservation. I inherited the high cheekbones. Mom was a lesbian warrior and community activist in South Central Los Angeles, who used her skills as a sharecropper's daughter to feed hungry blacks and Latinos by illegally planting fruits and vegetables in vacant lots that she used as community gardens to combat the food desert conditions of the inner city. The police were actually afraid of my mother, who never raised her voice louder than a whisper but commanded fierce authority.

I first started calling myself Vaginal Davis when I was 13, sexualizing the name of my idol Angela Davis. I was this strange-looking, sexually ambiguous child and lucky for me I was in the MGM program (Mentally Gifted Minors) in the LA Unified School District. Thank God in those days there was a social conscience, or I would have wound up like most minority children, either dead or in prison.

I was introduced to the punk scene by my older cousin Carla Duplantier, aka Mad Dog, the black Creole lesbian drummer of early punk band The Controllers. Carla was one of the first hundred punks in LA. One of the first places I ever performed was C.A.S.H. (Contemporary Artist Space in Hollywood), where the person on the door was Larry Fishburne from _The Matrix_ franchise, before he was famous. My first group was called The Afro Sisters and we were sort of an anti-band that sang a cappella. I wrote songs about the Black experience, mixing in Blaxploitation. I thought I was writing show tunes but somehow, the way it came out with my horrible singing voice, people viewed me as punk. Gays didn't get me at all. Only queer punks like Tomata du Plenty of The Screamers and Craig Lee of The Bags understood what I was doing. That's what led to me opening for punk bands and playing punk venues and art spaces.

Back then, gay clubs made people of colour and women show three pieces of photo ID for entrance. Plus that strange rule of NO OPEN-TOED SHOES ... in LA, a city with a warm climate. Bizarre. When I first started performing, _The LA Times_ would not even review my work. Then a bit later when they mentioned me it was always as 'V. Davis', as if the word Vaginal was somehow dirty and disgusting. It wasn't until _The New York Times_ printed my full name in a review in the early Nineties that the main daily paper in my own home town would spell out my full nom de plume.

In the 1980s I started organizing club nights. I had two really successful clubs: Club Sucker, a punque rock beer-bust and olde English tea dance, and Bricktops at the Parlour Club in the Russian quarter of Hollywood. I DJaned [_sic_] songs from the Tin Pan Alley era and performed and hosted live Weimar-style performances. This was right before I moved to Berlin.

My movie career? I started making these crazy underground video films. The most famous of the videos I did with Amoeba was 'That Fertile Feeling', which you can see on YouTube, where my Afro Sister Fertile LaToya Jackson gives birth to eleven-tuplets, then gets

REAGAN FIRES TEACHER

"She's a Commie!"

COURTHOUSE
KILLING
*Davis
Disappears!*

TERRORIST CHICK
GETS FRIED!
NIXON TO FBI
"Thumbs Up, Boys!"

Vaginal Davis, on the poster
for *Communist Bigamist:
Two Love Stories*, a theatre
performance in Berlin, 2012.

'I thought I was writing show tunes but somehow, the way it came out with my horrible singing voice, people viewed me as punk.'

VAGINAL DAVIS

on a skateboard. These films were not just low budget, they were no budget. At that time the gay and lesbian film festivals hated my films and would not screen them. Now my old insane films are collected by museums and film archives.

Back in the 1980s, my motto was move on to the next project, rarely looking back. That's why I don't have any copies of my old films, zines or records. I've never been a careerist or had business acumen. I never imagined that I would have an institutional art presence. When I left Los Angeles and moved to Berlin, suddenly I was rediscovered. People started to see me as a Berlin artist and not just some zany LA eccentric.

In my painting I use everyday items from the home, like makeup, nail varnish and witch hazel, because I am trying to expose the fact that fear and hatred of the profound sacred secrets embedded in all things femme is what propels gender violence and racial hatred in our world.

In my twenties and thirties I was still optimistic, thinking that I would meet someone eventually who I could have a relationship with. I've always considered myself a sexual repulsive because gay men were usually repulsed by me sexually and straight men, while at first titillated, would always wind up also rejecting me. Now, in advanced middle age, I am content that I haven't led a 'normative' life. Thank God I have a great therapist who helps me deal with all my tissues [sic] and in Germany I have kunstler insurance that pays for it all 100 percent, unlike in the States, where danger capitalism/advanced capitalism drains you of everything.

In 2012 I created a site-specific piece titled 'My Pussy is Still in Los Angeles (I Only Live in Berlin)', which I performed at the old Bullocks Wilshire department store. At NYU's Washington Square East Galleries I did a performative installation titled 'The Magic Flute: an Opera in Six Steps'. Holland Cotter of *The New York Times* singled it out as one of the best art events of that year. It was also the first project by my Berlin-based art kollektiv CHEAP in the USA. I joined CHEAP in 2001 with our first piece, CHEAP Jewelry, which saluted experimental filmmaker and performance artist Jack Smith and Hollywood sensation Carmen Miranda. For the last ten years I have curated and hosted a performative film event called 'Rising Stars, Falling Stars' that takes place at Arsenal – Institut für Film und Videokunst in Berlin.

Am I a drag terrorist? In 1996, I released a concept album with my punk-thrash band Pedro, Muriel & Esther, where I took on the made-up persona of Clarence Williams. a white supremacist militiaman from Idaho who is both racist and sexist, but started off life as a black queen having had a sex- and race-change operation, as if that is possible. Who knows, maybe now it is.'

Vaginal Davis – 2018

Bob the Drag Queen: crafty couture

As we have seen, the black drag queen effortlessly amplifies her fierceness with the aid of a unique, knowing wit. Bob the Drag Queen, for example, describes himself as an SLW, a 'Suspiciously Large Woman'. In the video for 'Purse First', Bob vamps through life proffering an evening bag as if it were an Olympic torch, embodying the get-off-my-runway tough humour that attends black drag. The fresh twist? Unlike so much of rap and drag culture which celebrates material excess, Bob's anti-designer hit song is a paean to thrifty crafting, its message made clear: you are an idiot if you blow money on a designer bag. Make it yourself, carry it with pride and enter a room 'purse first'.

Big Freedia: more bounce to the ounce

'I am not transgendered: I am just a gay male ... I wear women's hair and carry a purse, but I am a man. I answer to either "he" or "she"', states Big Freedia, who was born Frederick Ross in 1978. With her albums, TV appearances and tours, Big Freedia is a leading proponent of the New Orleans genre of hip hop known as bounce, which she popularized in an iconic contribution to Beyoncé's song 'Formation'. Called by some 'sissy bounce' (Freedia herself prefers plain old 'bounce'), its sexually aggressive lyrics are accompanied by a machine-gun bounce beat, sending fans into frenzied convulsions involving violent repetitive ass-shaking and twerking.

When she's not performing, Freedia operates an interior design business. In 2011 she was named Best Emerging Artist and Best Hip Hop/Rap Artist at the Best of the Beat Awards, and was nominated at the GLAAD Media Awards. That year she collaborated with RuPaul on a bounce song titled 'Peanut Butter'. With her Fuse reality show – *Big Freedia Bounces Back* – and her signature mannish delivery (she sounds like she's issuing commandments to a junkyard dog), fabulous Freedia has become a New Orleans folk hero.

Shangela: paying the rent

Despite being eliminated for her lack of sewing skills, Shangela made a big impact on the second season of *RuPaul's Drag Race*. The world was delighted when she and her 'Halleloo!' catchphrase blasted back on to season 3. In offices and shops across the land, girls named Angela suddenly found themselves redubbed Shangela or Shange. But would she have staying power? A decade later Shangela Laquifa Wadley, accomplished, professional and hilarious, and a shimmering standout of *RuPaul's Drag Race All Stars* season 3, is one of drag's success stories. Back in the last century, the black drag queen or trans woman was consigned to the scrapheap of life. Those of us who lived in New York in the 1970s and 1980s will not forget the dismal plight of the black trans hookers in the Meatpacking District. Mentored by RuPaul, Shangela Laquifa Wadley has rewritten the script. As New York-based drag-watcher and bon viveur Mechel Thompson noted, 'She bridges the gap between old and new drag, boomers to millennials. Shangela is a disciplined performer who is very much the NeNe Leakes of drag, brilliantly connecting with a very diverse audience.' Halleloo!

Latrice Royale: plus-size power

Eureka O'Hara, the self-proclaimed 'elephant queen', reeks of self-acceptance. Ginger Minj advocates 'solidarity with solid girls', and Kim Chi proudly describes herself as 'fat, fem and Asian'. The current reigning queen of drag queen fat positivity and self-acceptance, however, must surely be *Drag Race* alum Latrice Royale.

Timothy K. Wilcots was born in Compton, California, in 1972. After launching her drag career in the 1990s, she subsequently became an ordained minister and began performing same-sex unions. Royale was a supporter of marriage equality,

though she initially believed that it should not be called 'gay marriage', stating, 'I think it is special and unique. So why not identify and celebrate it as something special and unique, and not lump it in with the same thing that has been going on for years?' In 2018 she married longtime partner Christopher Hamblin in a gorgeously traditional wedding ceremony, announcing 'Bitch, I've had a change of heart!'

Black drag queens regularly refer to each other using words like 'ho' and 'bitch', and pastor Royale is no exception. According to Latrice Royale, bitch is a positive acronym: Being in Total Control of Herself.

The legendary children ... upcoming

Paris Is Burning transports the viewer back to a less tolerant, AIDS-ravaged New York City. The poignancy is unavoidable, especially as so many of the participants met untimely deaths. These queens of colour, brave, resilient and imaginative, lived comet-like existences. As Pepper LaBeija says, 'A lot of those kids at the balls, they don't have two of nothing. They don't eat. They come to the balls starving.' But Livingston's documentary is so much more than just a snapshot of another time. It subsequently became a drag blueprint, an anthem, a cultural artefact of massive significance for future generations.

It's impossible to imagine what the cultural landscape would look like had this movie not existed. Ball culture could so easily have evaporated into the ether. A million people walked past the voguers on the pier. Only one person, Jennie Livingston, had the presence of mind and imagination to pick up a camera and immortalize this subculture. A thousand creative people saw the voguers for the first time at Susanne Bartsch's first Love Ball, the AIDS fundraiser that took place at Roseland in 1989. Only one of the attendees had the imagination to hire them and take them on tour and put them in her video *and* her tour doc, *Truth or Dare*. And pay them. That person was Madonna.

Thanks to Jennie and Madge, the voguers appeared on Paris runways, TV chat shows and other venues. I vividly recall watching Willi Ninja and Adrian Magnifique voguing *à trois* with Iman on Thierry Mugler's Paris runway in the late 1980s. I myself repeatedly booked the House of Xtravaganza to perform at Barneys special events, including a rather naff fete honouring Sarah Ferguson and Prince Andrew, who were visiting New York on a trade junket. Unlike Queen Victoria, the royals were thoroughly amused.

Eventually, however, pop culture moved on. The aftermath was painful for the ball queens and the legends and the upcoming legendary children. They had been flung into the spotlight, and then watched as it slowly faded to black. It's undeniably painful when the circus packs up and leaves town without you. But now it's back. Voguing is enjoying a second wave thanks to choreographers like Trajal Harrell and ... drum roll ... to Kiki.

Voguing goes global, arriving in Vienna, the city of Strauss waltzes, at the 2013 Life Ball.

While Kiki has thrust voguing back into the spotlight, the glorious lingo of ball culture never went away. It is, in fact, louder and more creative than ever. The vernacular of the black drag queen now dominates the entire global world of drag. In many ways contemporary drag *is* black drag, with all its reading, realness, gagging and serving. And it's spreading. Just as the language and style of hipsterism and Beat culture – cool, far out, groovy baby, heavy man – slipped from black blues culture into common usage, so it is with black drag. Even CNN news anchors now talk about 'throwing shade'.

The black drag queen is the gift that keeps on giving. In addition to all of the above, she is now giving us something even more significant. The blurring of the old boundaries between trans and drag is an important next step in the evolution of drag, and the black drag queen – *quelle surprise!* – is leading the charge. As runner-up Peppermint noted at the grand finale of *RuPaul's Drag Race* season 9: 'Trans women have always contributed to the wonderful art form of drag. My contribution to drag is as powerful as any man.' Trans activist and *RPDR* alum, Monica Beverly Hillz put it even more succinctly: 'Drag is what I do. Trans is who I am.' Behold the black drag queen! Give her some walking room! Give her respect! Double snap.

Kiki is not a person, but rather a collective, a concept, a shape-shifting global voguing Bauhaus. The new ball culture is aggressive and politicized and tinged with rap and bounce. The aspirational categories such as Executive Realness and Opulence, a reflection of that 1980s *Dynasty* materialism, have been replaced by a stripped-down, assertive style. Duck walking and death dropping are the linchpins of this revival.

CHAPTER 5

Historical Drag

The arc of drag herstory is brutal, bizarre and laden with cautionary tales of madness and excess. Attention must be paid: 'Those who cannot remember the past are condemned to repeat it', declared philosopher George Santayana. With that in mind, I exhort you to learn your drag history, and learn it well, so that you might repeat only the most glamorous stuff and studiously avoid the gnarly bits. And, as I will clearly demonstrate, there is – brace yourself dear reader! – no shortage of gnarly bits.

Cross-dressing is a central theme in Euripides' play *The Bacchae*. Dionysus, the demented gender-disruptor, here played by Alan Cumming, persuades butch Pentheus to drag up as a maenad, an unhinged female follower of Dionysus. Lusting to see the maenads up close, and tantalized by the un-Greek notion of cross-dressing, Pentheus is drawn into Dionysus' reckless scheme, resulting in Pentheus' humiliation and death at the hands of his own mother.

Goddesses and monsters

Threads of transvestism are woven throughout the ancient cults. Slaying, in all senses of the word, is a huge part of mythology. When beauteous King Theseus arrives in Athens, he is mistaken for a girl and mocked by construction workers (we've all been there). He responds by flinging a chariot over the nearest house. Goddess Athena, born with the head of a man, wore genderfuck male armour over her frock. Achilles, the greatest warrior in Homer's *Iliad*, wore drag to avoid being hauled off by Odysseus to fight in the Trojan War. Aphrodite, goddess of love, was worshipped as a Venus Barbata (Bearded Venus) on the island of Cyprus.

Drag in Greek and Roman mythology represents everything from the loss or gain of power to erotic incontinence, disequilibrium and even punishment. Super-butch Hercules is enslaved by Omphale, the Amazon, as a reprisal for the murder of Iphitus, a bloke who Hercules believed had stolen his cattle. In a #timesup moment, Omphale compels Hercules, the epitome of masculinity, to wear drag and spin yarn, while she wanders about wearing a lion's skin and wielding an olive-wood club.

When Tiresias, the blind seer of Thebes, came upon two copulating snakes, he slayed them with a stick, which displeased the goddess Hera. In lieu of telling him to lip-synch for his life, she punished him by turning him into a woman for seven years. Sashay away.

Serving Egyptian realness and androgyny, Queen Hatshepsut ascended to the Egyptian throne in the fifteenth century BC. Since there were no pre-existing words or codes to indicate elevated status among women, Hatshepsut wore the traditional king's kilt and crown, along with a fake beard. Only by dragging up was she able to communicate her regal status.

Starting around 3000 BC, the Egyptian civilization kicked off thousands of years of mesmerizing mascara, entrance-making headdresses (see Nefertiti, Cleopatra and, subsequently, Liz Taylor in *Cleopatra*) and exit-making death masks (see Tutankhamun). Buckets of black eyeliner, figure-hugging floor-length shift dresses, towering headdresses encrusted with gold … and that was just the men. As King Tut clearly demonstrates, men and women got an equal shot at feminine adornment, resulting in a fiercely androgynous glamour that takes the breath away to this day.

In addition to its allure, drag also offered practical solutions. In ancient civilizations royal boys dragged up as girls to avoid being murdered by throne-hungry relatives. Women dragged up as monks in order to hide in monasteries, thereby escaping rape and pillage. Mulan, the legend of Han Dynasty China, dragged up as a boy to fulfil the family draft quota and save her father, and subsequently fill the coffers of Disney. Drag can be a real lifesaver.

Early drag, for regular folk, was often connected with religious rituals. As Camille Paglia has noted: 'The castrated, transvestite priests of Cybele, honoured in disco-like rites of orgiastic dance, survive in today's glamorous, flamboyant drag queens.' Paglia has also noted the global nature of drag, citing Syracusian men who were forced to perform initiation rituals while dragged up in Demeter's purple frock, and ancient Mexican women who were sacrificed and flayed so that male priests might wear their skin.

Classics scholars describe hordes of shrieking eunuchs, in wigs, makeup and garish female dress, roaming the towns of the ancient world, clinking cymbals and begging for alms. This phenomenon

Dionysus, the God of grape-harvest, ritual madness and religious ecstasy wore his beard with full drag, including tunics, veils, snoods and leopard skin. Very Conchita Wurst. Attractive women and satyrs with erect penises followed him everywhere, a testimony to the appeal of androgyny.

The eyebrows are working,
but where is the cheekbone
contouring? Meet Bacchus, the
Roman version of Dionysus, god
of madness, theatre, grapes and
more. Bacchus is here depicted
in all his blushing, guzzling
sexually ambiguous splendour,
by Caravaggio in 1595.

survives today with the fabulous hijras in India, outrageous groups of trans women and dragsters who enliven the streets of India, as they have done for centuries, rolling their kohl-rimmed eyes and cajoling money from passers-by.

While our society worships feminine beauty, Dionysian ancient Greece was riddled with masculine idolatry. The theatre occupied a massive space in the public consciousness, especially in fifth-century BC Athens, where legends like Aeschylus, Euripides, Sophocles and Aristophanes were churning out their *oeuvres*. With women mostly confined to the domestic arena, there were no female actors, and all the plays required male actors to cross-dress, playing Hecuba and Clytemnestra with the aid of masks, which sounds like a pain, but is probably easier than contouring and beating a lumpy, stubbled face with ancient home-made foundation.

Classical Greek theatre stipulated that only three actors be allocated to any given production. Unlike Peking opera or kabuki,

where the dragsters are chosen and trained for female impersonation, the Greek actor was obliged to switch back and forth between male and female roles. It was Electra one minute and Agamemnon the next. This had a positive effect: no actor could be stigmatized for taking on female roles.

The Romans absorbed Greek theatrical traditions, and made a number of modifications. They ditched the droning chorus, added painted backdrops, nude dancing, lowbrow comedies, animal acts and gruesome gladiatorial disembowellings. Violence and vice were in the house. As a result, the actors, all of whom were male and many of whom were wearing lady togas in order to play lady parts, were disdained and viewed as tawdry outcasts. Many were slaves who, if they turned in a lacklustre performance, would get beaten by their masters. Roman drag was, therefore, strongly associated with sleazy downtrodden luvvies. And then there were the emperors ...

left
John William Waterhouse, *The Remorse of Emperor Nero after the Murder of his Mother* (1878). Emperor Nero (r. AD 58–64) was totally kinktastic. He married a castrated boy, treating him as wife and empress, and acted in plays, enthusiastically taking on both male and female parts. When he wasn't murdering his mother Agrippina or burning Christians to provide ambient light at his parties, he was devising appalling sexual spectacles. In a Monty Python-esque gesture, he once masqueraded as a pregnant woman in labour. He even dragged up as a wild animal, and attacked the genitals of male and female victims who were tied to stakes, for his pleasure.

overleaf
Lawrence Alma-Tadema, *The Roses of Heliogabalus* (1888). Elagabalus ruled the Roman Empire from AD 218 to 222. His transvestite fantasies led to the desire for a sex change, and he had to be restrained from castrating himself. He offered half the Roman Empire to any surgeon who could equip him with female genitalia. This painting depicts his penchant for disposing of lovers by crushing them to death with rose petals.

Ancient Rome was, at the outset, democratic, idealistic and puritanical. As the empire aged, the rot set in and the real theatrics began, up at the palace. Emperor Caligula (r. AD 37–41), for example, lowered the tone with his psychotic depravities, and his adored frocks and wigs. When he wasn't organizing comic duels between disabled people, he was dragging up as Venus and seducing women, including his sisters. Tyrannical emperors made living theatre and performance art out of their appalling lives. Things went so awry that historians have speculated that lead plumbing rotted the brains of the high-ups. Drag played a significant role in this cavalcade of horror.

Emperor Elagabalus (Caesar Marcus Aurelius Antoninus Augustus) was so unsavoury he makes Caligula and Nero look like the Brady Bunch. Many figures in drag history practised 'class transvestism' – dragging up as a plebeian, or in Elagabalus' case, a prostitute. He would cruise the Roman brothels incognito, flaunting himself at all and sundry like a common tart. It should also be noted that Elagabalus' trans impulses were genuine: while the emperors Nero and Caligula were dragging up as part of a psychotic taboo-busting frenzy, Elagabalus' drag was an expression of his trans

Ciao Roma! Drenched in decadent androgyny, the 1969 film *Fellini Satyricon* depicts scenes from Petronius' *Satyricon*, a lengthy poem written during the time of Nero. Gluttons, gays and perverts vie for attention with an albino hermaphrodite.

What a strapping bride! Thor and Loki make an improbable bride and bridesmaid. In a ruse to recapture his hammer, Thor, mega-butch god of lightning and oak trees, throws on a bridal frock. Off he sets with his bro/pal Loki, dragged up as bridesmaid. They hit a bump in the road when Thor does something less than ladylike: he eats too much.

persona. Ellie had an additional rationale for his excesses: he used erotic spectacle to entertain and distract his adversaries in the hopes of reducing rivalries and bloodshed.

In Norse mythology, the relentless focus on machismo inevitably produces the occasional counterbalancing drag narrative. In addition to Thor and Loki (pictured above), we have Hagbard and Signy, the Romeo and Juliet of Norse mythology. At the denouement, hairy Hagbard frocks up in order to gain access to his beloved Signy. When her handmaidens start to wash and prep the mysterious visitor, they notice his hairy legs and raise the alarm. Hagbard is hanged, but not before witnessing the suicide of Signy. The moral of the story: forgetting to wax can have lethal consequences.

Lady Macbeth has a penis

The Renaissance was a groovy, swinging period of creative expression and new ideas. Despite the cultural flowering, the Christian Church maintained an unforgiving position regarding the role of women, and the evils of cross-dressing. Fortunately for us, biblical and legal prohibition failed to eradicate drag. *Au contraire.* Drag sought refuge in the theatre where it flourished as never before. Ladies and gentlemen, I give you the Elizabethan theatre of William Shakespeare, where all the roles were played by men. Why not simply assign the roles to cis women? Drag is ungodly, but not as ungodly as allowing women to prance about onstage in front of a vulgar rabble.

Were they any good? Scholars have frequently questioned the merits of assigning emotionally complex sensual roles such as Cleopatra and Ophelia to fresh-faced young men. A.M. Nagler, writing in 1958, suggests that lads got around this by 'acting stylistically', in other words playing a woman *as if* playing a woman. As we shall see when I touch on kabuki and Peking opera, stylized drag-acting discourages the audience from taking a literal view of gender and from asking too many questions about what's under that frock. Stylized, melodramatic performance can also

Mark Rylance plays Olivia in an all-male production of Shakespeare's *Twelfth Night*, directed by Tim Carroll at the Apollo Theatre in London in 2012.

'Shakespeare knew what he was about when he worked so much sexual ambiguity into his characters, but too often it has been lost with women in the roles that he'd envisaged being played by young men in drag.'

TIM WALKER reviewing *Twelfth Night* in *The Telegraph*, 2012

prove emotionally powerful (as demonstrated by Gloria Swanson in *Sunset Boulevard*).

As noted in Glamour Drag, drag has a maturing effect on the wearer: after maquillage and hair and feminine artifice, the scrappy youths of *RuPaul's Drag Race* transform into *femmes du monde*. With a bit of padding and extra rouge, a 16-year-old lad might give a convincing portrayal of a 26-year-old woman at the height of her erotic powers. It is also good to keep in mind that Shakespeare was drawing on a larger pool: Londinium. It is safe to say there were 'it' lads – the Panti Blisses, Shangelas, Danny La Rues and Coccinelles of yesteryear – ready and willing to take on Cleopatra, without, hopefully, turning her into *Carry On Cleo*.

Shakespeare was constantly assessing the effectiveness of his cross-dressed 'female' leads, as evidenced by the fact that he repeatedly uses drag as a narrative device. This goalpost-moving strategy no doubt prevented audiences from fixating on whether a particular actor was 'passing' effectively. The most extreme example occurs in *As You Like It*. When Rosalind and Celia do a runner, the former drags up as 'Ganymede' in order to become a protector. Shakespeare then has 'Ganymede' dress as a woman to help a male chum, Orlando, in his pursuit of Rosalind, while at the same time fending off the amorous intentions of Phoebe. Audaciously, Shakespeare has given us a man (the actor), dressing as a woman, dressing as a man, dressing as a woman.

A word about the drag itself: according to detailed descriptions, the stage frocks were Elizabethan and very posh, which means ruffs, corsets, hoops, farthingales and slashed sleeves. There was no attempt to evoke ancient Rome or Egypt (remember Cleopatra's request to have her laces – corset slats – cut?). These heavy garments were sold to the theatre by the servants of the upper classes (the notorious Sumptuary Laws of the day prevented the servants from wearing these discarded garments themselves). These majestic frocks added greatly to the general spectacle, but inhibited physical movement. Some believe that it was under these circumstances that the term 'drag' first slipped into the vernacular. The dragginess of drag was emphasized when the actor in question ditched his frock in favour of his tights and man-drag and began leaping about the stage.

Dorothy Minto as Nerissa and Alexandra Carlisle as Portia giving lawyerly realness in a 1910 production of *The Merchant of Venice*: girls dragging up as men, in girl roles that were previously assigned to boys. It's all so confusing.

While many of the principal actors were celebrated – Edward Alleyn, Richard Burbage, William Kempe – the same cannot be said for the dragsters. They lived in fear of their voices breaking, an event which, thanks to poor diet, occurred in the late teens. Some sources claim the ladyboys died young, poisoned by the lead toxicity of their white maquillage.

Sun King or Selfie King? Louis
XIV wearing Apollo drag for a
performance of the Ballet de la
Nuit in 1653. Keep in mind that
Louis was the macho one –
wait until you meet his brother.

Louis XIV's Drag Race

Shakespeare died in 1616, thereby missing the dawn of the nelliest period in history: the Baroque. The flowering of the Baroque period – early seventeenth to late eighteenth century – brought us ornate styles in painting and dress. European buildings from this period, with their hallucinogenic embellishments, resembled drag queens caught in tornados. With their satin frock coats, lace mouchoirs, powdered wigs and novelty beauty marks, the aristocratic men of the Court of Versailles got seriously in touch with their feminine sides.

Anne of Austria was married to French monarch Louis XIII. In 1683, after several stillbirths, she managed to produce an heir, Louis XIV. Two years later she gave birth to another lad, who was christened Philippe, duc d'Orléans. She raised Lou to be more butch and entitled than Phil, a strategy intended to avert potential rivalries. Whatever she did, it seems to have taken. While his brother Louis always strived to demonstrate masculine bravery – he famously endured an operation for an anal fistula without so much as a squeak – Philippe got in touch with his feminine side.

'Monsieur', aka Philippe, duc d'Orléans, in a frock, as portrayed in the 2017 series *Versailles*.

below

Gender-binary pioneer the Chevalier d'Éon alternated between mumsy gowns and military uniforms. As a legacy, non-homosexual transvestism has been described subsequently as 'eonism'.

above

François-Timoléon, abbé de Choisy. During childhood, little François's mother always dressed him as a girl. This practice continued and by age 18 his waist was 'encircled with tight-fitting corsets which made his loins, hips, and bust more prominent'. His uninhibited delight in the exploration of his female identity is remarkable for its candour and enthusiasm: 'I have heard someone near me whisper, "There is a pretty woman". I have felt a pleasure so great that it is beyond all comparison. Ambition, riches, even love cannot equal it.'

MADEMOISELLE de BEAUMONT, or the
CHEVALIER D'EON.
Female Minister Plenipo. Capt. of Dragoons &c.&c.

This eighteenth-century engraving captures the titillation and bewilderment generated by the cross-dressing bravado of the Chevalier d'Éon.

The duc d'Orléans was the party-planner par excellence of Versailles. He helped his brother, the Sun King, construct and maintain the intoxicating carousel of distractions and indulgences that was the Court of Versailles, thereby kettling and defanging the French aristos and keeping them under his thumb. In the court the King's brother was known simply as 'Monsieur', which in retrospect seems a little shady, especially given the fact that he adored diamonds and rouge and regularly frocked up. Paradoxically it was Philippe, not Louis, who distinguished himself on the battlefield, albeit while slathered in bijoux and maquillage.

As the women's clothing of this era became more elaborate and costumey, so the inclination of men to wear it increased. In a gossipy memoir chock-full of unsparingly honest self-disclosures, the French aristocrat François-Timoléon, abbé de Choisy (1644–1724), left us detailed descriptions of his drag: the pages rustle with speckled black satin, white damask underskirts and tasselled muslin shawls. And then there are his beauty regimens: 'The gown revealed my shoulders which always remained quite white through the great care I had taken with them all my life: every morning I lathered my neck with veal water and sheep's foot grease, which made the skin soft and white.'

Charles-Geneviève-Louis-Auguste-André-Timothée Éon de Beaumont (1728–1810), usually known as the Chevalier d'Éon, was a French diplomat, soldier and spy for Louis XV, who successfully infiltrated the court of Elizabeth, Empress of Russia, dressed as a woman. In 1771 the Chevalier declared that, though raised as a man, he was in fact a woman and lived as such from that point on. Posted to London she created a *scandale fou* with her passion for fencing (in a frock and bonnet) and overspending, inspiring wagers on the Stock Exchange to determine her gender. On her death it was discovered that her body was anatomically male.

Pirate of the Caribbean, Anne Bonny.

It wasn't just the men dragging up around this time. Female-to-male drag could solve a multitude of problems and create opportunities. The social and physical mobility denied to women was just a jerkin away. But does that necessarily entail becoming a pirate? Bastard child Mary Read (1685–1721) was dressed as a boy by her mother in order that she might impersonate a deceased brother, enabling mater to gain access to an allowance, while Anne Bonny (1702–82) was dressed as a boy by her father in order that she might become a lawyer's clerk, a job that was unavailable to a girl. Both women concealed their gender and became pirates. They ended up in a triangulated relationship with a swashbuckler named 'Calico Jack' Rackham, and predictably all three ended up in the clink. Rackham was hanged, and tough-talking Bonny's final comforting words to him were, 'had you fought like a man, you need not have been hang'd like a dog'. Bonny herself got a stay of execution because she was with child and was later released. Read, who also claimed to be pregnant, died in prison of a horrid fever.

Drag went increasingly on the record in the eighteenth century. The commentators of the day took note of characters like the Chevalier d'Éon, and of the mysterious vamping, camping flotsam that began to pop up on the increasingly bustling streets of Europe. Drag was now connected with all kinds of unsavoury stuff, most notably the crime of homosexuality, which was punishable by hanging. In London the focus of attention for police and gossiping lampoons were the notorious molly houses, a gay/trans subculture of clubs and brothels. These establishments, filled with cross-dressing gays and others, became subjects of scandal, none more so than Mother Clap's Molly House. Raids were common, and defendants were dragged before the authorities in all their finery. In the words of one contemporary account: 'Next morning they were carried before the Lord-Mayor in the same dress they were taken in. Some were compleatly rigg'd in gowns, petticoats, head-cloths, fine lac'd shoes, furbelow'd scarves and marks; some had riding-hoods; some were dressed like milk-maids, others like shepheardesses with green hats, waistcoats and petticoats; and others had their faces patch'd and painted, and wore very extensive hoop-petticoats, which had been very lately introduced.'

Punishment was unimaginably severe and might well include hanging. At the very least the dragsters were guaranteed public humiliation and violence in the pillory and stocks, which often resulted in serious injury and death. After her trial Mother Clap, the fun-loving landlady who loved nothing more than to carouse and gossip with her clientele, was pilloried in Smithfield Market – she collapsed repeatedly under the barrage of stones and refuse – and then imprisoned. It is not known whether she survived imprisonment.

While Mother Clap was being pelted with filth, the courtly life of Europe continued its brave struggle against ennui. Weapons against boredom included gambling, boozing, eating bonbons, hunting, dancing, singing and prancing about in outrageous

There was nothing unisex about the eighteenth-century Brits. Men's attire was butch and militaristic. Women's fashions were ornate and romantic in the extreme. The gendered nature of clothing added massively to the frisson generated by cross-dressing, even if it's just trying on the wife's lacy bonnet.

A MORNING FROLIC, or the TRANSMUTATION of SEXES.
From the Original Picture by John Collet, in the possession of Carington Bowles.

416   Printed for & Sold by Carington Bowles, at his Map & Print Warehouse, N°69 in S¹ Pauls Church Yard, LONDON.   Published as the Act directs

costumes. Opera had the ability to combine any or all of these. The development of this profoundly camp art form, complete with elaborate sets, costumes and dance numbers, was inevitable. And so was castration.

Stefano Dionisi plays the adored castrato Farinelli in the 1994 movie of the same name.

Like in rock music, audience adulation was most frequently directed at the lead singers, especially the castrati. The castrated youths who sang soprano and mezzo roles – the Church forbade women to undertake such ungodly pursuits – were admired for their beauty and their commitment. Opinions vary about their singing, detractors likening the results to scalded cats and shrieking peacocks. Nonetheless Scalzi, Caffarelli, Nicolini and, most famously, Farinelli were the Madonnas and Gagas of the genre. As historian Philip Core notes: 'hysterical, spoilt and outrageous, they covered themselves with jewels and led furiously partial cliques. Travesties of nature as well as dress, they reigned in society as freaks who retained a magic power through the beauty of their voices.'

By the 1780s the castrato craze was falling out of favour, especially in Britain, where it was seen as morally degrading and allied to effeminacy. Women began to perform the roles and proved compelling and irresistible, especially when they began to take on the romantic male leads. Pants roles, trouser roles, travesty roles – call them what you will, they welcomed legions of songstresses to the stage, delighting audiences with their playful male impersonations and their soprano and mezzo-soprano duets. Examples include Cherubino in Mozart's *The Marriage of Figaro* (Cherubino, dressed as a girl to avoid army duty, is played by a woman, who plays a man who dresses as a woman), and Siebel in *Faust* and Hansel in *Hansel and Gretel*. When a male character needed to seem strange or mysterious – Orpheus, for example, in Gluck's *Orpheus and Eurydice* – the role was written for a woman in drag. In a world of hoops and paniers, the sight of a woman in tight breeches and figure-hugging attire was not without sizzle. The combo of glamour and sexual uncertainty embodied in the pants roles was, and is, intoxicating to both men and women. The eternal allure of androgyny!

The last great pants role burst onto the scene in 1910 with Richard Strauss's *Der Rosenkavalier* and the godlike drag king Octavian. A beautiful, chivalrous young man with an older aristocratic lover, this berouged drag king spawned a thousand ceramic figurines and chocolate box designs, and a million panto dandinis.

below
Drag is central to the plot of Beethoven's 1822 opera *Fidelio*. Leonore disguises herself as a man in order to spring her husband from false imprisonment. As with many of Shakespeare's plots, Leonore's drag adds plot complexity and an erotic frisson.

'The operatic castrati are the forebears of present-day drag artists.'

PHILIP CORE

Peking opera

Scholars trace the origins of Chinese theatre, now known as Peking (or Beijing) opera, back to 1050 BC. Its development is hard to track owing to China's size and the obliterating effects of various conflicts. During the reign of the Qianlong Emperor (r. 1735–96) women were banned from theatre troupes for reasons of morality. Enter the *tan*, the young bloke who looked halfway decent in cheongsam. In order to convince the audience of their gender, these actors developed a stylized version of femininity. An exaggerated vocal delivery became the cornerstone of drag performance. First-time viewers of Peking opera are invariably shocked by the otherworldy screech that characterizes 'female' acting. Over time, several specialized genres of *tan* evolved, including modest obedient *tan*, fearless vigorous martial arts *tan*, and malicious evil *tan*.

opposite

An actress impersonating a female impersonator. The ancient female *tan* roles of the Peking opera are now played by cis women, who must work hard to adopt the stylized versions of their gender bequeathed to them by centuries of actors in drag.

right

In 1924 Mei Lanfang was voted China's most popular actor. He was emblazoned across commemorative stamps. His drag artistry was emulated not only by men (in frocks), but also by contemporary female performers.

Kabuki theatre

In my opinion, the greatest drag artist of all time is Tamasaburo Bando, the most celebrated *onnagata* and Living National Treasure of Japanese kabuki theatre. I have seen Tamasaburo perform on multiple occasions while on work trips to Japan in the 1980s and '90s, when my colleagues were so charmed by my enthusiasm for this centuries-old art form that they even arranged for me to go backstage and watch the actors getting dragged up and slapped up. Chills.

Tamasaburo combines a stupendous theatricality and exaggeration – those costumes! – with breathtaking subtlety. For the uninitiated I suggest binge-watching on YouTube: 'Wisteria Maiden', 'The Maiden at the Dojo Temple', 'Yamanba'. His ability to walk in ten-inch black lacquered clogs, executing backbends and figure-of-eights with each foot – and shuffling duck walks – is unsurpassed.

Like Peking opera, kabuki theatre also underwent a protracted dithering about whether men or women should play female roles, and as usual the women got the short end of the stick. In 1628 women's kabuki was banned because the actresses – all female – had become associated with prostitution. The men took over, forming all-male troupes known as *wakushu* ('young men's') kabuki. The female roles were given to attractive men whose charms, subsequently, proved irresistible to certain samurai. In 1652 *wakushu* was banned and replaced by *yaro* ('mature male') kabuki. Butch haircuts with shaved foreheads became the norm for men. The tradition of adult men playing women's roles – the *onnagata* – was established and a new and astonishing genre of stylized femininity was created. The rules of gesture, dress, makeup, deportment and vocals were set down by a famous eighteenth-century *onnagata* named Yoshizawa Ayame. An unwitting proponent of method acting, centuries before Strasberg, he/she instructed actors to think, feel and react as women in their daily lives.

Japanese National Treasure Tamasaburo Bando. The traditions of kabuki drag are rigid and centuries-old, but the visual bravado of the end product still delivers a punch. It is easy to see where the Japanese avant-garde fashion of the last half-century comes from.

Eventually, the ladies get their own back! Sort of. The Takarazuka Revue, founded in 1914, is a Japanese all-female musical theatre troupe – there are multiple troupes operating at any given time – currently selling two and a half million tickets a year. The audience comprises young girls and middle-aged women, many of whom weep during performances. Actors play either male or female roles – never the twain shall meet – in the lavish productions of Western-style musicals, and, occasionally, shojo manga and Japanese folk tales. The women who play male parts are referred to as *otokoyaku* ('male role'), while those who play female parts are *musumeyaku* ('daughter's role'). The *otokoyaku* are the locus of fandom. Emotional crowds bearing cakes and gifts greet the suavely butch 'male' leads as they enter and leave the stage door.

During my sojourns in Japan I enjoyed the lowbrow kitsch of Takarazuka. The earnestness and unwitting corniness of the shows makes Disney seem avant-garde. The *otokoyaku* in particular exude a romance-novel heroic demeanour without a shred of irony. Takarazuka approaches gender playfully and with a total disregard for 'heteronormative' concerns. They seem not to be commenting on gender at all. The results are earnest, deeply camp, and well worth the price of entry.

The drag kings of Takarazuka live as men and use male pronouns. The Takarazuka brand – wholesome, romantic and heartwarmingly innocent – is anxious to distance itself from gender politics and anything 'unsavoury'.

Drag gets modern ... and then postmodern

Our historical drag journey starts to wind down in the late nineteenth century, as the modern age of drag dawns. During the gay 1890s, referred to by historians as the Mauve Decade, drag becomes a *thing*, with a name and a reputation to uphold. Drag then jumps into her Ford Model T and begins to speed up, heading towards the Jazz Age and beyond. But every so often drag looks in the rear-view mirror and returns to the arc of history as a source of inspiration.

Nostalgia has always been connected with drag. Throughout the twentieth century, history was viewed by drag performers as a giant gender-inclusive dressing-up box, just waiting to be plundered. In the Swinging Sixties drag queens at the Vauxhall Tavern would parody World War II wartime spirit by lip-synching to Gracie Fields. The Golden Age of Hollywood inspired the drag queens of the post-War era. In order to give us the Egyptian effect, Pepper LaBeija looked back 3,000 years. In the 1980s, Bette Bourne of Bloolips took brooms, milk crates and garbage, and gave us a deconstructed Marie Antoinette court costume, complete with paniers.

below left

In 1892 *Charley's Aunt*, a drag farce in three acts written by Brandon Thomas, broke all historic records. The protagonist is a young hooray named Lord Fancourt Babberley – Babbs to his friends – who drags up in order to play the role of chaperone for his pals. The play became a massive global hit, and film and musical adaptations followed. It marked a watershed moment for drag.

below right

Sir Frederick Ashton and Sir Robert Helpmann serving baroque bitchiness as the Ugly Sisters in a 1960s production of *Cinderella* at Covent Garden.

MR. W. S. PENLEY.—"Charley's Aunt."

right

Pansexual French actress Sarah Bernhardt (1844–1923) slept in a coffin, made love in a hot-air balloon and wore a live lizard around her neck tethered by a gold chain. In 1901 she dragged up as Napoleon II in *L'Aiglon*, a play written especially for her by Edmond Rostand. You can listen to a 1910 recording of her emoting her way through a performance, in trilling French. She makes no attempt to butch up her voice – I felt I was listening to Hyacinth Bucket, yelling over the garden fence *en français* – which must have added significantly to the dragtastic nature of her performance.

L'AIGLON   Sarah Bernhardt

P BOYER Phot.

3690

opposite

Freddie Mercury gets medieval. Henry Cyril Paget reigned as the 5th Marquess of Anglesey from 1875 to 1905. Nicknamed 'Toppy', his lordship was a reckless drag-addicted spendthrift who blew the equivalent of half a billion pounds on jewels, historical costumes and decadent living. He was known for dragging up and entertaining guests with 'sinuous, sexy, snake-like dances'. Unsurprisingly, Toppy kicked the bucket without producing an heir.

But history is not all thigh-slapping pastiche and nostalgia. To study the arc of civilization is to be drenched in blood, madness and brutality. Drag and trans, always vulnerable to shifts in politics, have often felt the cat-o'-nine-tails. We are currently living in an era of relative tolerance where the acceptance and visibility of drag and trans have surged dramatically. Masculinity is in retreat and gender nonconformity is on the march. Will it last? Some scholars point out that drag and trans have surged in late-stage civilizations – Babylon, Greece, Rome, the Mauve Decade of Oscar Wilde, Weimar Germany – and that this freewheeling exploration of identity was immediately followed by sharp decline and total collapse. Hopefully the prominence of drag and trans in our society is not an augur of doom, but rather a sign of the arrival of a progressive utopia that will last for eternity. Fingers crossed.

Historical Drag

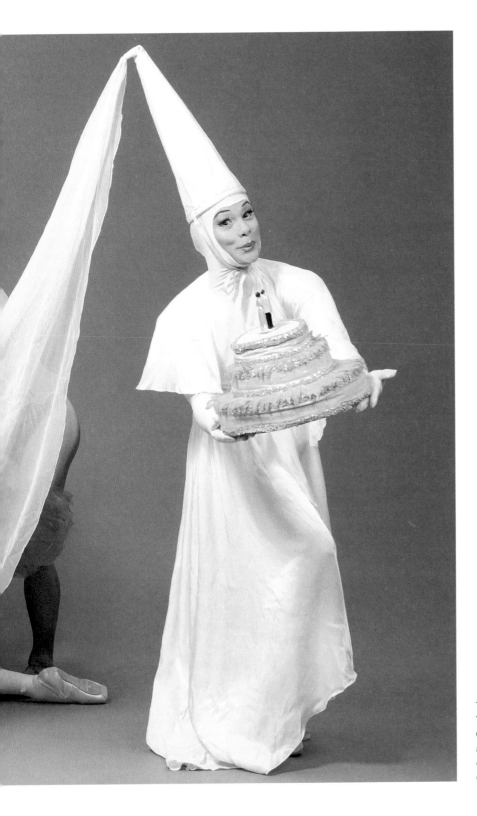

The all-male Ballets Trockadero de Monte Carlo has been mocking and magnifying the campy conventions of nineteenth-century ballet since 1974.

CHAPTER 6

Comedy Drag

The field of comedy drag is vast and enduring. Why is it so successful? Why are we amused? Is it what Freud dubbed 'the laughter of unease'? If so, then what, pray, are we all so uneasy about?

At the start of this book, I suggested that glamour drag is underpinned by our fear of female nature, as embodied by the myth of Medusa, the lethal diva, the castrating dominatrix. Most often worn by gay men, glamour drag sizzles with taboo notions of fierceness, seduction, sadism and destruction. Comedy drag, in sharp contrast, is less Medusa and a lot more Medea – the mythological mother who took revenge on her unfaithful husband by murdering her own children. Comedy dragsters, I would suggest, riff on the notion of a critical controlling mummy, an irate mummy, a homicidal mummy.

Channelling Barbara Cartland. Since her season 6 win on *RuPaul's Drag Race*, Bianca Del Rio has laboured tirelessly to establish herself as the reigning empress of comedy drag. Her whip-smart insult humour would have made Joan Rivers very happy: 'On the celebrity food chain, I fall somewhere between Bethenny Frankel and the midget on *Game of Thrones*. For now, it's a good spot to be in. I'm famous enough that I can get good dinner reservations, cut lines at airports and park in disabled parking spots.'

Comedy drag zeroes in on our ambivalence about maternal control, and lets rip. According to Camille Paglia, men 'have only a brief season of exhilarating liberty between control by their mothers and control by their wives'. She notes that transvestism is far more common among men 'because it originates in the primary relation of mother and son'. Since the drag queens of comedy historically have been mostly heterosexual men, one suspects there might well be an element of misogynistic revenge at play.

When I was in my twenties, I distinctly recall a vogue for theme parties, the two most common being 'vicars'n'tarts' and 'come as your mother'. My straight male friends would need a few drinks in order to wriggle into their girlfriend's tarty bustiers and garter belts, but to drag up as mother they would have to drink the entire bottle. Norman Bates was right: for better or worse, a boy's best friend *is* his mother.

'When you're in drag, it's your licence to kill, because you are the butt of the joke.'

TRIXIE MATTEL, winner of *RuPaul's Drag Race All Stars* season 3

Tyler Perry based his beloved character Madea (almost Medea!) on his own strong-willed mother: 'She would beat the hell out of you but make sure the ambulance got there in time to make sure they could set your arm back.'

As he developed the character of Dame Edna, comedian Barry Humphries took inspiration from British Prime Minister Margaret Thatcher, surely one of the most terrifying matriarchal symbols of the twentieth century. Edna adopted Maggie's famous slogan of 'caring and compassion', and subverted it: 'My mother used to say that there are no strangers, only friends you haven't met yet. She's now in a maximum security twilight home in Australia.'

Off with her head!

Comedy drag sprang from a desire to disarm the nightmarish female archetypes of Victorian England (think of the angry queens and sadistic child-beating duchesses in *Alice in Wonderland*). Strict governesses, relentless nags, ruler-wielding schoolteachers and cruel stepmothers have all provided great fodder. In addition to the obvious psycho-therapeutic benefits of nag drag, there was also a practical component: it was far easier for a portly middle-aged comic to impersonate an ugly matron than to resemble a beautiful woman (glamour drag would come later).

The genre owes much to the collision of two separate institutions. On one side we have the respectable theatre of Oscar Wilde and Gilbert and Sullivan, producing tyrannical grandes dames like Lady Bracknell (Wilde's *The Importance of Being Earnest*) and the gruesome and predatory spinster Katisha (Gilbert and Sullivan's *The Mikado*). At the other end of the spectrum we have the music halls. While the theatre was the destination of polite society, the same cannot be said of the music halls, where bawdy comics with knobbly knees – Harry Randall, Herbert Campbell, Dan Leno et al. – donned skirts, frowzy wigs and mumsy shawls and brayed double entendres

We are not amused! Less of a sumptuous drag queen, more of a queen in sumptuous drag, the ultimate disapproving matriarch, Queen Victoria, cast a long, puritanical shadow over late nineteenth-century England, unwittingly fuelling the bawdy drag-strewn irreverence of Victorian music halls.

'An ugly baby is a very nasty object – and the prettiest is frightful.'

QUEEN VICTORIA

Frowzy yet fabulous, Fred Emney, Harry Fragson, Harry Randall and Walter Passmore illuminate a 1907 pantomime production of *Sinbad*.

Grotesque, malevolent and gaudy, the pantomime dame is a drag comedienne's dream. Lee Mengo and Brian Hibbard unleash their respective ids as the Ugly Sisters in a Welsh production of *Cinderella*.

Dan Leno as 'the Baroness' in the pantomime *Cinderella* at the Drury Lane Theatre, London, in 1896. Dan Leno was a beloved English comic panto dragster, famous for his clog dancing, his alcoholism and his wretched untimely demise.

at well-lubricated working-class audiences. It was inevitable that a certain porosity might develop between the freewheeling music halls and the establishment theatre, as creative types would happily sample the delights of both. So what do you get when you mix haughty dowagers with bawdy chaps in frocks who will do anything for a laugh? Panto drag!

A British institution, the pantomime is a show aimed at children and families that erupts in theatres across the UK around Christmas. Commonly based on a popular fairy tale or nursery rhyme, the genre is characterized by songs, jokes and slapstick humour. Although panto hit its stride in the nineteenth century, its origins had been percolating for centuries. Antecedents include the marketplace storytellers of the ancient world, the Mummers of the Middle Ages, the *commedia dell'arte* of sixteenth-century Italy and the Harlequinade. Panto has always had a dodgy whiff about it: even in ancient Greece the *pantomimus* was known for its sexy jokes and the effeminacy of the participants. In its British incarnation, the panto is one of the most drag-strewn of theatrical genres and remains popular right up to the present day.

Soldiers in skirts

The first half of the twentieth century was bookended by two World Wars. The in-between years were convulsed by advances in communication and entertainment – the decadent Jazz Age, the yammering telephone, the speeding car, the glamour of art deco, the goddesses of the silver screen. This was a period of dizzying progress, which had a huge impact on gender and comedy drag, not to mention eyebrow shaping and frock design.

Douglas Byng, star of more than 25 pantomimes, loomed large on the cultural landscape in Britain at this time. Suave, witty and sophisticated, Byng also fitted perfectly into the glamorous world of 1920s and 1930s cabaret and revue, for which Byng wrote many Coward-esque sketches with titles like 'Doris, the Goddess of Wind' and 'I'm the Pest of Budapest'.

The silent movies of the era were another perfect vehicle for comedy drag, by its nature very much a sight gag. Charlie Chaplin, Buster Keaton and Laurel and Hardy all frocked up, looking grotesque and frumpy in the process. Drag was less prevalent in the subsequent early talkies, where deep voices and a sharper focus rendered the ruse more sinister than funny.

Wartime encourages gender fluidity. Women wear trousers and men, in a desperate attempt to distract their comrades from the unfolding bloodbath, wear frocks and perform improvised theatricals. Nobody needed a laugh more than the brave soldiers in the First World War trenches.

Though Douglas Byng is credited with moving magnanimously between working-class pantomimes and snooty cabaret, he remained relentlessly snobby about which parts he would play, preferring regal dowagers over scullery maids. His sherry-drinking genteel posturings were revisited in the 1970s by a drag duo named Hinge and Bracket.

World War II dragsters were nothing if not versatile: one minute you were blowing kisses at your bunkmates through bee-stung lips, the next you were side by side, attempting to save the free world.

The Second World War saw a marked increase in enthusiasm and tolerance for drag. Shelley Summers, a contributor to Kris Kirk and Ed Heath's landmark book *Men In Frocks*, joined the Royal Air Force in 1944: 'Combined Services Entertainment were looking for people to do drag, as there were only five women soldiers in the whole place. Anybody who did it got sergeant stripes immediately.' With or without a promotion, the drag queens of World War II were happy to play dress-up with kindred spirits, though the realities of conflict were ever-present, and many recall performing in front of dying or disfigured amputees. The vigorous drag culture did not end on VE Night. Like many post-War drag queens, Shelley Summers found work in the touring all-male revues – *Soldiers in Skirts!* – that remained popular until the mid-1950s.

The great comedy drag explosion

The returning troops brought home their enthusiasm for drag and somehow infected the entire population. I have a snap of me and my best pal in our backyard in Reading in the 1950s. We are in full drag. It was taken by my mother.

It is no exaggeration to say that, once the telly started to appear in British living rooms, we Brits began to drown in drag. Some performers, like Danny La Rue or Foo Foo Lammar, were professional female impersonators. Others, such as Dick Emery, Stanley Baxter and Benny Hill, were straight-but-camp comedians, hugely popular TV personalities, who regularly dragged up in order to generate cheeky-but-family-friendly primetime laughs. In *Monty Python's Flying Circus*, the most famous and influential British TV comedy series of the twentieth century, the 'women' were grumbling housewives, homicidal grannies, puritanical enemies of the Permissive Society. The show's only real women were presented as vacuous dolly birds, there to look sexy and giggle occasionally.

below
TV star Dick Emery created his own recurring characters, the most popular being a breathy lady named Mandy, a homage, many posited, to Mandy Rice-Davies, an audacious figure at the centre of the Profumo scandal. Mandy's catchphrase – 'Ooh! You are awful. But I like you' – is still heard today. Vigorously heterosexual, Emery was married five times.

right
Stanley Baxter endeared himself to legions of British fans impersonating icons such as Judy Garland and Bette Davis. His *pièce de résistance* was his impersonation of Elizabeth II. Baxter was married to the same woman for 46 years.

While the Brits drowned in drag, the Yanks had to make do with more occasional fare. Bob Hope, Milton Berle, Paul Lynde and Jerry Lewis all gave it a whirl, but the puritanical discomfort with homosexuality – unschooled in panto culture, large swathes of the US assumed that a man in a frock must be an ill-intentioned pervert – kept comedy drag to a minimum in popular culture. The one exception was Flip Wilson and his beloved character Geraldine. In 1970 Wilson won a Grammy for his album *The Devil Made Me Buy This Dress*.

Beginning in the 1960s, gay culture came screaming out of the shadows, with drag following close on its heels. As gay bars, pubs and discos proliferated, so did the number of performing drag queens. These were not your family-friendly Dick Emerys and Stanley Baxters – this new wave of drag queens was angry, loud, proud and foul-mouthed. Years of repression created the need to let off steam, to curse, to mock, to shock and to frock. The rude and fabulous creativity and comedic talent that gushed forth during this period of new-found freedom is remarkable.

Many drag comedians structured their humour around certain catchphrases. Geraldine, aka Flip Wilson, popularized 'When you're hot you're hot; when you're not you're not' and 'The Devil made me do it!'

The Vauxhall Tavern, with its bawdy low-budget drag performances – lip-synching to Vera Lynn, Shirley Bassey or Dusty – holds a special place in my heart. I was there in the early 1970s, on the night that right-wing skinheads flung bricks through the window. We kept calm, and carried on … having a fabulous time.

At this time drag became more gay, and more postmodern. The homosexual obsession with the glamorous, often tortured female entertainers of stage and screen – Judy Garland, Mae West, Bette Davis, Marilyn, Liz – began to seep into comedy drag. Arcane Hollywood references – a drag queen dressed as Joan Crawford wielding an axe from the movie *Strait-Jacket*, or possibly just a vignette from Joan's own life when she ('Mommie Dearest') commanded her children to help her chop down the rose bushes – brought gay audiences to paroxisms of knowing joy. Medea was in the house, and she was more lethal and glamorous than ever.

Pubs and bars in working-class neighbourhoods, with their low rents and minimal policing, were perfectly poised to become gay bars and, as a result, drag venues. Financial outlays were meagre or non-existent. The gents' toilet doubled as the changing room; a couple of handheld spotlights and a free pint were offered to the 'lady' in the frock, if you were lucky. In other words, *every expense was spared*. Many noteworthy talents made a name for themselves in this gritty milieu, including Adrella, The Playgirls, The Harlequeens and Regina Fong in the UK, and Craig Russell and Charles Pierce on the other side of the Atlantic.

Amid the cheap gold lamé, beehive wigs and tacky lashes of 1960s and '70s Medusan drag queens lurked a comedic anomaly, the fabulous Mrs Shufflewick, star of The Black Cap pub in Camden Town and other venues. Her patter often began with a reference to her moth-eaten fur stole: 'It cost two hundred pounds. Didn't pay for it meself. I met two hundred fellas with a pound each.' What could be more tawdry than a mother figure who turns tricks? Mrs Shufflewick shuffled off her mortal coil in 1983, but has gone on to reach posthumous cult status.

Not only were pub drag queens forced to change 'in the bog', they were also often obliged to use the bar as a runway, scampering up and down, snatching tips and desperately trying not to knock over customers' beers and Babychams. The new clubs and discos on both sides of the Atlantic, on the other hand, were a great deal safer and more sanitary, and they offered the ultimate luxury: *a proper stage, with spotlights.*

Comedy drag proliferated and became hipper and more self-aware. Inspired by the arty recklessness of Warhol superstars like Holly Woodlawn and Jackie Curtis, the drag comedians of The Pyramid Club dreamed up performances and skits that were unconventional, creative and hilarious: Hapi Phace, Billy Beyond, Tabboo!, Lady Bunny, Sister Dimension, Ebony Jett, Linda Simpson, and so many more. As drag began to shed some of the old-school showbizzy clichés, clubs like The Pyramid proliferated across Europe and America.

Mrs Shufflewick, aka Rex Jameson (1924–83), picked up where music hall drag left off and created his own comedy genre of working-class granny drag.

opposite
Sage, political pundit, founder of Wigstock, the savagely hilarious Lady Bunny is an enduring and beloved mega-force in the world of drag. Her noteworthy success is attributable to her ability to combine comedy and glamour, as exemplified by her monstrous wigs.

'I told RuPaul to act her age . . . and she died.'
LADY BUNNY

Artist, East Village free spirit and drag artist Tabboo! – aka Stephen Tashjian – created the iconic and influential artwork for The Pyramid Club and Wigstock.

Broads on (and off) Broadway

As comedy drag gathered momentum the inevitable happened: theatre drag. Some of it was on Broadway, and some of it was more than a little off. Witty, clever individuals, theatre luvvies and thespians with a passion for stagecraft spawned new genres and spoofed old ones.

Bloolips

Peter Bourne (front row, second from the left), graduate of London's Central School of Speech and Drama, was destined for a conventional career in the theatre. In the 1970s he joined a Gay Lib commune, changed his name to Bette Bourne, and founded Bloolips – Bette Bourne, John Brown, Lavinia Co-op, Diva Dan, Gretel Feather, Jon Jon, Naughty Nickers, Precious Pearl – a merry band of self-deprecating nellies. With their hastily applied slap (makeup), found objects, thrift-shop drag and their floor mop wigs, they were the antithesis of today's fierce and glamorous 'look queens'. As Lavinia Co-op recalls, 'We weren't wearing tits, we didn't always have wigs, we were wearing white face, we were doing fantasy colours and glitter and shapes. You weren't impersonating women ... you're coming from drag and opening a door to somewhere else, ... finding another way.' The result was a kinder, messier, less misogynistic drag.

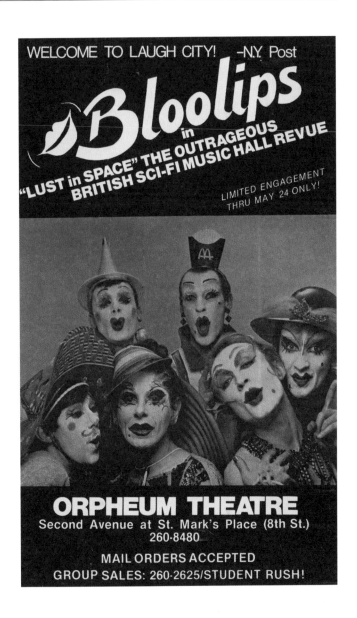

Charles Ludlam

Many performers began to explore more legitimate outlets. In order to get longer theatre runs and serious reviews, drag comedians needed scripts, costumes, lighting and direction. Charles Ludlam took the ad hoc creativity of pub and club drag and combined it with the manic farce of Feydeau, creating razor-sharp comedic parodies of various theatrical sacred cows including *The Ring Cycle*, *The Satyricon* and *Camille*. Ludlam's Ridiculous Theatrical Company included longtime collaborators Everett Quinton and Black-Eyed Susan, and produced endless hours – 29 plays! – of postmodern drag-drenched insanity, which live on in the comedic gay memory today. Ludlam died from AIDS-related complications in 1987.

Divine

Divine scored a theatrical hit on both sides of the Atlantic with a very un-PC spoof of 1950s prison movies titled *Women Behind Bars* (produced by Ron Link and writer Tom Eyen). Divine played a cruel, dykey wardress, clearly inspired by Hope Emerson's portrayal of the sadistic matron in the 1950s movie *Caged*. This play was followed up with another memorable production, this time set in a strip joint, titled *The Neon Woman*. Comedy drag was shifting gears, repurposing female-oriented entertainment – melodramatic movies that sincerely attempted to highlight women's struggles – and relentlessly mocking them.

Charles Busch

Charles Busch, drag queen, playwright and visionary – and the most successful theatrical drag comedienne of the 1980s and 1990s with a groaning shelf-full of awards – embodies the postmodern impulse to pastiche all aspects of female cinematic melodrama. His most famous and long-running production was *Vampire Lesbians of Sodom*, described by *The New York Times* as having 'costumes flashier than pinball machines, outrageous lines, awful puns, sinister innocence, harmless depravity'.

Lypsinka

In a category all his own, we have John Epperson, aka Lypsinka, star of Wigstock, pub, club, theatre and Paris runway. Epperson broke boundaries between the lowbrow and the highbrow. Like Busch and Ludlam, Epperson soaked up the melodrama of the silver screen and catapulted it back at his salivating audiences in a postmodern frenzy. Nobody who has seen Lypsinka do his manic telephone performance will ever forget it. During this electrifying skit Epperson responds to multiple invisible jangling telephones, lip-synching along with edited audio clips from movies, histrionic moments of cinematic female despair and rage. By day Epperson worked as a rehearsal pianist at the American Ballet Theatre. Epperson brought the precision and drive of the world of ballet to the creation of Lypsinka. John has also written (and performed in) two musicals, *Ballet of the Dolls* and *Dial 'M' for Model*, and a screwball farce that was inspired by the Medea myth – there she is again! – titled *My Deah*, which debuted Off-Broadway in 2006.

More trans people are entering the entertainment world, producing a new kind of humorous subtlety that is informing drag and trans. These individuals seem less inclined to hide behind the postmodern pastiches that fuelled comedy drag during the second half of the twentieth century. Drag queens no longer need to hide behind a Carmen Miranda costume. This evolution is epitomized by Justin Vivian Bond, a transgender, Tony-nominated entertainer who goes by the gender-inclusive they/them/their. Their performances are infused with a subtle melancholic humour that seems to accurately reflect and reveal their own personality. Justin Vivian Bond has inhabited a variety of looks and identities, including Kiki DuRane, one half of the queer-core, post-punk cabaret duo Kiki and Herb. As Kiki DuRane, they relied more heavily on postmodern pastiche. As Justin Vivian Bond they is themself.

Today, as more and more trans comedians and entertainers take the stage, the face of comedy drag is changing. The bawdy raging postmodern campy humour of pub, club and disco is morphing into something more subtle and emotionally real. Younger millennial audiences have never seen a Maria Montez or Joan Crawford movie, so those pastiches and parodies that delighted my generation would fly right past them. The new gender-inclusive generation responds to the realness and emotional vulnerability of groups like Denim and elegant thoughtful chanteuses like Justin Vivian Bond.

Comedy drag wakes up

below left
As Lily Savage, Paul O'Grady took pub drag mainstream in the 1990s. His massive television success – 'I dress up as a middle-aged prostitute and do a game show' – reflected the Brit fondness for a particular archetype: the loud-mouthed tart with the heart and the leopard slacks. In the era of #metoo, this genre of slag drag does not resonate with younger audiences, and Mr O'Grady MBE has brilliantly reinvented himself as the British face of animal rescue, sans frock.

below right
Matt Lucas took the most appalling aspects of antisocial teenage behaviour, added a tight ponytail (a Croydon facelift), a Bristol accent and a name: Vicky Pollard. Famous for her 'yeah but no but yeah' catchphrase, Vicky became a *Little Britain* favourite.

Back in the 2000s, Matt Lucas and David Walliams made a big impact with their caricatures of British archetypes on the BBC comedy series *Little Britain*. Their romping grotesques drew big ratings and mixed reviews. Writing in *The Independent* in 2005, Johann Hari criticized *Little Britain* for sketches that 'hinge upon the ugliness of female flesh, and barely a woman is shown without the actors playing her being padded into monstrous fat-suits. It's hard to escape the conclusion this is a gay man's woman-hatred with a laughter track, a sketch-long recoil from breasts and vaginas'. Tyler Perry, aka Madea, has faced similar criticism. Is it time for comedy drag to pivot?

The face-slapping movie queens of film noir no longer resonate with young audiences. The tyrannical mommies and unforgiving Lady Bracknells that propelled comedy drag in the early years are no longer relevant, for the simple reason that those gorgons and governesses no longer exist. In short, the world has become a kinder, gentler place. We live in a society where women

share parenting duties with men. Kids skip off to school without the fear of corporal punishment administered by rage-filled war widows. Wellness rooms and equality are the *mots du jour*. In the era of #metoo, misogyny-based comedy is no longer everyone's *tasse de th*é. Alongside today's glamour queens, look queens and bawdy, brash Biancas and Shangelas, a fresh and progressive flock of drag comedians is migrating away from the sardonic, the cynical and the foul-mouthed. Their message is one of inclusivity, creativity and empowerment.

In the past, the targets of comedy drag were frequently overbearing women. Now, increasingly, they are becoming overbearing and treacherous men. Misogyny has been replaced by a vibrant misandry. As a result, it is a great time to be a drag king. Previously unique, New York comedy drag king Murray Hill is now spawning many imitators. Not since the early twentieth century have so many drag kings found the spotlight. As noted in Butch Drag, some drag king performers, like Adam All, eschew toxic masculinity in favour of a suave gay metrosexual identity. Others jump right in with both mock-croc loafer-clad feet and take on the toxic dudes.

Melissa McCarthy performed a gum-chewing, tour de force takedown of former Trump press secretary Sean Spicer in 2017.

The Trump presidency has proven to be a red rag to a drag king. *Saturday Night Live* has seen Melissa McCarthy give good Sean Spicer (pictured) and Kate McKinnon portray Jeff Sessions, while Rosie O'Donnell had indicated her willingness to drag up as Steve Bannon, before he got fired. Trump is, allegedly, not a fan of these drag king satires because he 'doesn't like his people to look weak'. The latter statement reveals, dramatically and unequivocally, that drag – in particular the effrontery of drag king comedians who dare to emasculate his top guys – is getting under the president's skin. Comedy drag is doing its job.

'I came out here to punch you in the face, and also . . . I don't talk so good.'

MELISSA MCCARTHY as former Trump press secretary Sean Spicer

CHAPTER 7

Popstar Drag

T he average American male is terrified of being stared at. For most of the twentieth century the guiding principle for mens' clothing design was anonymity, with one notable exception: popstars. In order to sell records, the male popstars of the conservative American mid-century needed fans to take notice, and a sure-fire way to stand out was to raid the feminine repertoire. Elvis wore gold lamé suits and caked his lashes with mascara. Little Richard sang 'Tutti Frutti' under a towering pompadour and face-full of pancake makeup, and James Brown sported midriff-baring chiffon blouses. Condemnation rained down. Notoriety was achieved. Records were sold.

In 1984 Queen released the single 'I Want to Break Free', accompanied by a video for which all the band members dragged up in a loose parody of *Coronation Street*, with a bit of Nijinsky + nudity thrown in. Though well received in the UK, the video was banned by MTV. In 2011 a meta moment occurred when Katie Price, aka Jordan, dragged up as Freddie in drag, complete with moustache, at the *Let's Dance for Comic Relief* benefit.

In 1969, two days after the
death by drowning of the
group's founder Brian Jones,
The Rolling Stones put on a
freebie show in Hyde Park,
London. Mick Jagger wore a
Byronic frock, read a poem by
Shelley and released a small
cloud of white butterflies (the
cloud would have been larger,
but a significant number of the
butterflies croaked in transit).
Many mistook Mick's drag for
a Victorian christening robe. It
was, in fact, a hot-off-the-rack
item designed by Swinging
Sixties designer Michael Fish,
part of his 'dresses for men'
concept. Each garment at Fish's
emporium bore a label that read
'Peculiar To Mr. Fish'. The client
list included a blond bombshell
named David Bowie who wore
a silk brocade Fish frock on
the cover of his 1970 album
The Man Who Sold the World.

Five minutes ladies! Jimi Hendrix, Mitch Mitchell and Noel Redding – The Jimi Hendrix Experience – fighting for the mirror. Seattle-born Hendrix moved to London in late 1966 and took full advantage of the exploding unisex sartorial freedoms.

Across the pond, the Brits – The Stones, The Kinks, The Yardbirds, The Beatles – took popstar drag and turned up the volume. What better way for working-class lads to kick against the stuffy British establishment and the class system than by dressing like a bunch of decadent girls? The boys were encouraged in their flamboyance by a select and influential group of homosexuals, such as gallery owner Robert Fraser, interior designer Christopher Gibbs, Brian Epstein (manager for The Beatles), Robert Stigwood (Cream and Bee Gees), Simon Napier-Bell (The Yardbirds, Marc Bolan), Billy Gaff (Rod Stewart) and Ken Pitt (David Bowie). These gay Svengalis were drag enablers: *we can't run around London with our eyes rimmed with kohl, trailing silk foulards and fringed manbags and driving a vintage Rolls painted with psychedelia, because we are gay and gay is verboten, but you can, because you are a young straight popstar!* (Homosexuality was eventually legalized in the UK in 1967, but gays remained *personae non gratae* in many quarters.)

The 1970s: golden age of frock rock

The popstars of the 1960s had created a safe space where taboos could be broken, and the post-Hendrix lads of the new decade took full advantage. Billowing bohemian blouses and cascading tresses became the norm. Boys wore girls' skimpy knits and crop tops with unisex crushed-velvet bellbottoms. Ladies' accessories – fedoras, tam-o-shanters, feather boas, bangles and necklaces, vintage or ethnic silk foulards – were piled on with gypsy-ish abandon. The emerging popstar drag was nothing if not radical.

Back in 1968 Marc Bolan, a pretty, Jewish attention junkie from Hackney, and drummer Mickey Finn had formed a band called Tyrannosaurus Rex. The group's first album featured the longest and fey-est title in rock history: *My People Were Fair and Had Sky in Their Hair ... But Now They're Content to Wear Stars on Their Brows*. In 1970 Tyrannosaurus Rex became T. Rex and Marc Bolan abandoned the psychedelic folk genre – goodbye hippy bohemia, hello camp costumery – and joined the glam-rock revolution, pumping out hit after catchy hit: 'Ride a White Swan', 'Hot Love', 'Get It On', 'Jeepster', 'Telegram Sam', 'Metal Guru' and more. By this time Bolan's girly glam-rock style was so extreme that rumours abounded that he was embarking on a sex-change op.

While Marc Bolan went stark raving pop, vamping and pouting his way into mega popstardom, others pushed glam rock in a more sinister, edgy, less commercial direction. *Aladdin Sane, Low, Station to Station, Pin Ups* ... David Bowie's astounding output was always lurid, mysterious and meticulous. From *Hunky Dory* to *Scary Monsters*, and right up to *Black Star*, the product was always *considered*, as was Bowie's extraordinary androgynous style.

For me it all started at the Finsbury Park Rainbow on 20 August 1972. Bowie, channelling his Ziggy Stardust alter ego,

Marc Bolan's iconic Seventies look – corkscrew tresses, top hat, boa and glittery cheeks – inspired generations of male and female performers from Slash to Stevie Nicks to Cher to Twisted Sister and now Kesha.

The man who sold the world, and bought a dress. Wearing Mr. Fish, Bowie adorns the lawn of Haddon Hall, the Victorian villa in south London where he and wife Angie lived from 1969 to 1971.

strode through this historic performance – aided and abetted by Lindsay Kemp (see page 53) and his mime troupe – wearing a series of extraordinary creations by designer Kansai Yamamoto. It would be inaccurate to describe Bowie's look as gender-neutral. With his slender elegance, he looked like a beautiful extraterrestrial female, with extraordinary leadership skills. Bowie was regal, and in charge.

A word about Bowie's high heels: today women wear outrageously theatrical shoes while men, even fashionable men, have to make do with normcore sneakers or boring flat-soled lace-ups. Today's shoes are, in other words, stuck in the gender binary. Not back then. Back in the 1970s we were all dreaming of a unisex utopia where men and women overcame their vast differences by dressing alike. During the Ziggy years girls wore outrageous platform shoes – metallic snakeskin boots designed by Mr Freedom or Terry de Havilland – *but so did we dudes.* My favourite pair was an electric blue scaled-up version of a child's sandal with a massive chunky platform.

opposite
Bowie was living proof that getting tarted-up imbues the wearer with power and invincibility, even if the outfit in question is a Kansai Yamamoto twinkle-knit unitard with one leg and one arm missing.

Popstar Drag

above
The New York Dolls used drag to emphasize a reckless, anarchic, masculine belligerence.

above right
Bowie and Bolan spawned legions of glam-rock dragster followers, with delightfully mixed results. Like many of their cohorts, The Sweet resembled good-natured bricklayers dragged up for Halloween by their adoring wives.

Popstar drag, though repellent to the establishment, proved to be catnip to female fans. The non-threatening sensitive bloke in the satin, sequins and kohl gave women permission to pick up the reins, and they did. Bowie's band The Spiders from Mars were initially reluctant to sign on to the whole platforms-and-glitter thing, until they saw the effect it had on girls.

While glam-rock drag sat well on pretty boys like Bowie, Bolan and the members of Roxy Music, it was less successful on others. Many lads recklessly jumped on the drag bandwagon, their brawny masculinity straining at their satin seams. While popstar drag emphasized Bowie's elegant androgyny and de-emphasized his testosterone level, the same cannot be said for others. Drag and mascara rendered them more blokey, and hokey. Examples include Slade, Alice Cooper, Iron Virgin and Gary Glitter.

opposite
Bearing more than a passing resemblance to Marlene Dietrich in *Shanghai Express*, ambient music king Brian Eno back during his tarty Roxy Music years.

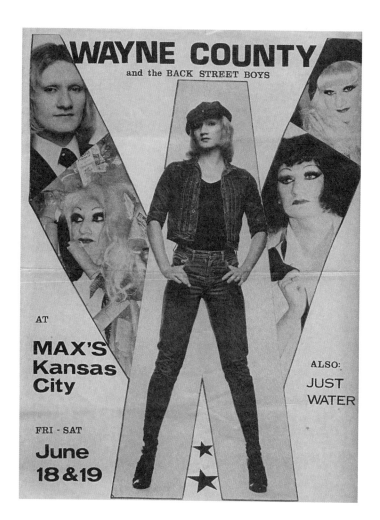

Wayne/Jayne County's impressive résumé includes taking part in the Stonewall riots and playing the part of the Lounge Lizard in Derek Jarman's punk movie *Jubilee*.

Drag was largely anathema to the 1970s earthquake that was punk, with one very important exception: Wayne County – rock's first openly transgender performer – who eventually changed his/her name to Jayne County. Performing with The Electric Chairs, County recorded some noteworthy punk songs including 'Man Enough to Be a Woman' and 'Fuck Off'.

Meanwhile, the number of black performers who embraced the prevailing popstar drag in the 1970s is small. Earth, Wind and Fire, Sly Stone and George Clinton of Funkadelic were costumey and over the top, but studiously avoided anything girly. One name alone shines like a mirrorball in the darkness: the great Sylvester, the androgynous gay icon with the church-lady falsetto, and a one-time member of the Cockettes (who we will meet in Radical Drag). His version of Stevie Wonder's 'Living for the City' is a thing of beauty, a wrenching anthem for all black drag queens and trans women.

opposite
Sylvester scored massive hits with 'You Make Me Feel (Mighty Real)' and 'Do Ya Wanna Funk'. He died of AIDS-related complications in 1988. His funeral in San Francisco was a massive cultural event. Opting for an open casket, a perfectly maquillaged Sylvester bade farewell to weeping fans wearing a gorgeous red kimono.

The multi-talented Joey Arias
– cabaret artist, drag queen,
Billie Holiday impersonator,
Warhol and Dalí lookalike –
personifies the post-punk
postmodern sophistication
of the new wave era. In 1979
a strange drag trio famously
performed on *Saturday Night
Live*: David Bowie belted out
a track from his album *Station
to Station* titled 'TVC 15', aided
and abetted by Joey and

performance legend Klaus
Nomi. Arias recalls: 'Bowie's
management handed us $1,000
cash. We were gagging. Klaus
snatched up the black Thierry
Mugler tunic dress at Henri
Bendel. I did the same, in red.
David's management thought
the whole drag thing was
too forward and shocking.
Not David. Inspired by us,
he ordered a Chinese airline
stewardess outfit for himself.'

The 1980s: androgyny à la mode

The 1970s gave us glam rock, disco and funk, and, as if that wasn't enough, the decade concluded with a giant cultural enema in the form of punk. Though otherwise unconventional in every way, punk was not drag-friendly, Wayne/Jayne County being the lone standout (see page 172). While drag was largely anathema to the genre, the punk makeup styles – I am thinking in particular of Debbie Harry, Siouxsie Sioux and Nina Hagen – have proven influential to subsequent drag queens. Maquillage aside, punk's most important gift was the creation of a blank slate. The brutality and madness of the Sex Pistols et al. eradicated all pre-existing ideas about music, design, fashion and graphics. Liberated by punk, pop music experienced an explosion of unbridled creativity – The Psychedelic Furs, Joy Division, The Specials, U2, Depeche Mode, ABC and more – and fresh, increasingly fashionable expressions of popstar drag.

Annie Lennox has said she enjoyed the powerful feeling of dragging up and standing shoulder to shoulder with Dave Stewart, her suited collaborator and former lover. Lennox has explored the joys of cross-dressing throughout her career. In her famous 1992 video for 'Why', she transitions from fresh-faced boy to gaudy drag queen.

Grace Jones sang of feeling like a woman and looking like a man, as she stalked the stage in butch Giorgio Armani suits, looking like a pissed-off commandant from an alien galaxy.

opposite
Boy George was a central character in the street-style phenomenon known as The Cult With No Name, or the New Romantics. It was foppish costume for foppish costume's sake.

Emerging from the post-punk scene of the New Romantics, Boy George gave history one of those 'where were you' moments. Where were you when you first clocked a picture of pretty made-up George, in his oversized hat, his beribboned extensions and his Sue Clowes-designed muumuus, and learned, to your great surprise, that this lipsticked coquette was actually a bloke? I was in a record store on Melrose named Vinyl Fetish. Having been around transvestites and transsexuals my entire life, I always prided myself on my trans radar. But I was totally had, and totally smitten.

Though relentlessly modish, affable George navigated the pop world with the unpretentious charm of a Vauxhall Tavern drag queen. When in 1983 he and his band picked up his Best New Artist Grammy, he addressed his fans: 'Thank you, America. You've got taste and style and you know a good drag queen when you see one.'

So much more than a Marilyn impersonator, Marilyn, a pal of Boy George, used his beauty and impudence to carve out a pop niche. His 1983 appearance on *Top of the Pops*, performing his hit 'Calling Your Name', is seared into the national consciousness. The phrase 'gender bender' – loathed by George and Marilyn – slipped into common parlance at this time.

Naff alert: the 1980s also saw the return, and repackaging, of hairy hard rockers. The hair metal genre took classic hairy rock styling – think Robert Plant or Jethro Tull – and updated it for the age of aerobics. The hippy locks were replaced by torrents of moussed New Jersey housewife hair, tarty makeup, Tanfastic and Lycra. This genre enjoyed explosive popularity with straight audiences: proponents include Twisted Sister, Def Leppard, Whitesnake, Poison, Bon Jovi, and a chart-topping Christian rock band named Stryper (pictured).

Not every 1980s 'gender bender' was big on humour. Steve Strange's popstar drag grew out of the New Romantic tradition, a style that relied heavily on sucking in your cheeks and not laughing at all. Steve's hit 'Fade To Grey' – the band was named Visage – was a rhythmic dirge for all the working-class kids who had discovered the fine art of sulky posing while wearing esoteric costumes. I can say that because I was one of them. Look for me in the video for Kim Carnes's 'Bette Davis Eyes'.

Piratical chic, for both men and women, was big in the 1980s. Vivienne Westwood designed an entire collection celebrating all things pirate and opened a store that resembled a listing ship. Adam Ant and a group named Bow Wow Wow were the foremost proponents of this unexpected gender-inclusive genre. And Pete Burns, lead singer of Dead or Alive, gave us the world's first drag pirate.

In 1985 Dead or Alive rocketed to Number One with 'You Spin Me Round (Like a Record)'. It was a hit in 48 countries. Pete's subsequent celeb journey saw him appear to transform, surgically and sartorially, from a drag queen in a pirate blouse to a full-on woman. But the truth is more elusive. In 2006, after multiple plastic surgery debacles, Pete made a comeback as a contestant on *Big Brother*. He entered the BB house looking like a brunette Patsy from *Ab Fab*. During filming he surprised his housemates when he declared, in his deep Scouse voice, 'I think of myself totally as a man'.

With his unpretentious Liverpudlian working-class affect, Pete Burns endeared himself to a wide audience, the majority of whom have never seemed to question the fact that he was a bloke who presented as a glamorous woman.

The future looks fecund

Since the glory days of the 1970s and 1980s, there have been few drag mega popstars like Boy George and Pete Burns. Those seeking old-school popstar drag in the 1990s and 2000s looked instead to the Eurovision Song Contest, and were usually not disappointed. This annual festival of gloriously naff pop, easy to mock but never boring, has consistently broadcast a message of LGBTQ tolerance. In 1998 a trans woman from Israel named Dana International made history by winning the competition, thus ushering in a new era of Euro trans inclusivity.

In 2007, Verka Serduchka, a futuristic Ukrainian Dame Edna in Cazal eyewear, sang 'Dancing Lasha Tumbai', an infectious ditty in multiple tongues, and achieved second place in the Eurovision Song Contest.

Today, this inclusivity has spread way beyond the realm of Eurovision. While the rapidly evolving drag/trans scene can be rather confusing, even for the initiated, this world is astoundingly creative and fertile. Speaking in 2017, on the eve of his third Fischerspooner album launch, Casey Spooner, no stranger to frocks, clarified the unclarifiable: 'What's happening right now that's so amazing is that nothing has to be so clear ... There's a place for everyone, like a garden.' A gorgeous wild, tangled, mysterious garden.

With the face of a Kardashian and the beard of a French nineteenth-century poet, Conchita Wurst, the Austrian Eurovision entry from 2014, wowed the audience with her powerful voice, narrow hips and her rendering of 'Rise Like a Phoenix'. Her seemingly mythological victory – Dionysus also paired tunics and veils with a full beard – have made her an icon for global trans acceptance.

Singer–songwriter Shamir is
emblematic of the growing
non-binary scene. Of his
androgynous voice, he
says, 'It's not feminine, it's
not masculine. It's a happy
medium ... I feel like if the
world was more like that, our
problems would be gone.'

Today's popstar garden is redolent with the influence of classic drag queen drag. As Michael Musto noted in 2014, 'LGBT culture is more prevalent than ever right now, so it's more common to liberally borrow from it and even pretend you're a contestant on *Drag Race*, vagina notwithstanding.' Female artists like Beyoncé, Nicki Minaj and Rihanna incorporate the exaggerations and hyper-femininity of drag queens into their styling. Miley and Gaga express solidarity by claiming trans status. The female popstars of today, Swift, Perry and Lovato, concoct an elaborate restyled persona with every new album, à la Ziggy Stardust.

Drag, in varying degrees and genres, is thriving in today's pop culture landscape, with one notable exception: the boys. Those headlining male popstars are not dragging up the way they used to in the days of Jagger, Bowie and Burns. 'Gender bending' would appear to hold no allure for big performers such as Drake or Bruno Mars. Even out gay Sam Smith remains sartorially conservative. Drag, for straight male performers, has lost much of its transgressive frisson. Nobody is going to lock you up for wearing a frock. In these trans-positive times you would be lucky if anybody noticed. And nobody is going to high five a hetero dude for frocking up *unless he actually means it.* Dragging up purely for attention or dough would, in our era of increased sensitivity, be viewed as less than respectful.

CHAPTER 8

Movie Drag

'Fasten your seatbelts. It's going to be a bumpy night', declares Margo Channing, played by drag icon Bette Davis, in the movie *All About Eve*. As we explore the history of celluloid drag, Davis's famous line seems more than applicable. The history of movie drag is all about extremes: shrieks of laughter or screams of terror.

Drag cameos popped up hither and thither in the early years of cinema, mostly in the context of comedic farce – the Marx Brothers did it, as did Charlie Chaplin, Jerry Lewis and Laurel and Hardy. All that changed in 1959 when director/writer Billy Wilder grabbed comedy drag by the brassiere and hoisted it onto the big screen and into the global consciousness. He cast Marilyn Monroe, Jack Lemmon and Tony Curtis in *Some Like It Hot*, concocting what was to become the most beloved movie of all time.

Conservative mid-century America was stunned by the notion of male leads in frocks, but ultimately fell for *Some Like It Hot*'s Daphne (Lemmon) and Josephine (Curtis) once it became clear that these fellas were not unsavoury perverts, but rather reluctant dragsters, forced to cross-dress to elude marauding criminals in the Roaring Twenties.

Wilder, a sophisticated soul who witnessed first-hand the drag-strewn decadence of pre-War Berlin and Paris, was unable to resist adding a little extra provocation to the movie's denouement. The famous final scene shows a frustrated Jack Lemmon tearing off his wig and 'fessing up to suitor Osgood Fielding III, played by Joe E. Brown. 'Nobody's perfect', responds Osgood, immortalizing a line that adorns Wilder's tombstone. The happy consenting males boat off into the sunset.

One year later: a man in drag yanks back a shower curtain and stabs a naked woman to death, and nobody is shrieking with laughter. The shrieks of terror are provided by the famous Bernard Herrmann soundtrack. Off camera, a sound-effects person plunges a knife into a casaba melon to simulate the stabbing sound. You are watching Alfred Hitchcock's *Psycho*.

Psycho not only became the most watched horror movie of all time, it also forged in the public consciousness a strong connection between drag and homicidal insanity. Hitchcock replaced the thigh-slappingly funny with the blood-curdlingly sinister. You want to scare the crap out of an audience? Put the lead male in a frock and play it straight. In the ensuing decades, drag careened back and

In *Psycho*, Anthony Perkins plays Norman Bates, a son so consumed with love for his mother that he kills her, mummifies her and then dons her limp house-dresses.

WARREN

EMILY

PLAYED BY

JEAN ARLESS

above

A year after *Psycho* was released, horror maestro William Castle released *Homicidal*, a *Psycho*-lookalike that featured a strange twist: instead of a son dragging up as a mother, we have Jean Arless, playing both brother and sister roles. Perhaps sensing that the movie was more campy than scary, Castle offered his audiences a gimmick: 60-minute 'fright breaks' that allowed people time to leave the theatre and regain their composure.

right

More Freudian mommie stuff: in 1968, Academy Award winner Rod Steiger starred in an Oedipal wigfest titled *No Way to Treat a Lady*. How might misogynist psychopath Christopher Gill (Steiger) rid New York City of its population of ageing broads? Donning multiple wigs and disguises, he embarks on a city-wide throttling spree. Inexplicably, one of his victims is a trans woman.

forth between terror and farce. This era of dragsploitation was propped up by an increasing public awareness of psychotherapy and psychoanalysis. What causes a man to frock up? His love/hate relationship with mommie of course.

In 1976 Roman Polanski directed and starred in *The Tenant*, a disturbing film that highlights xenophobia and reinforces that *Psycho* connection of drag to the horrors of mental illness. Polanski plays Trelkovsky, a young man who moves into a dismal Paris apartment. He discovers that the previous tenant, Simone Choule, an Egyptologist, attempted to kill herself by jumping out of the window. Simone, in full body cast, languishes in a grim Paris hospital ward. When good-natured Trelkovsky visits the paralyzed stranger, she lets out a blood-curdling howl, and later dies. Depressive, taunted by neighbours and increasingly obsessed with the previous tenant's fate, he starts to unravel. As proof that Trelkovsky has finally lost it, he starts to drag up as Simone.

Roman Polanski wigs out in a vintage-style floral dress, in the gruesome finale of *The Tenant*, a homage to the un-gay side of Paree.

In *Dressed to Kill* (1980), A-lister Michael Caine takes the drag psychodrama one step further when he plays both a shrink and a transvestite slasher. His trenchcoat-and-shades drag recalls the sadomasochistic fashion photographs of Helmut Newton that were popular at the time. When Hitchcock learned that director Brian De Palma intended *Dressed to Kill* as a homage to his movies, he replied, 'You mean, fromage'.

Meanwhile, below ground, the avant-garde was having a love affair with drag. During the second half of the last century, drag became a staple of 'alternative' movies by such directors as Jack Smith, Rosa von Praunheim and Rainer Werner Fassbinder. What was unsavoury and objectionable to a mainstream audience – as we've seen, drag was acceptable only as laughable slapstick or the prelude to a homicidal bloodbath – was given a warm and rousing reception in the art houses of yore.

The most drag-committed underground film director was undoubtedly Andy Warhol. He famously said, 'If everybody is not a beauty then nobody is', opening the door to the notion that even a drag performer with stubble and a crappy wig should be seen as an object of beauty. Warhol, along with his cinematic collaborator, director Paul Morrissey, showcased the marginal drag queens and trans women in their orbit and packaged them as 'superstars'. Oozing hooker street style, Holly Woodlawn, Jackie Curtis and the glam-but-dentally-challenged Candy Darling enlivened various Warhol/Morrissey movies, such as *Flesh*, *Trash* and *Women in Revolt*, not to mention their immortalization in the Lou Reed anthem 'Walk on the Wild Side'. Warhol's genius was to plonk these unconventional attention junkies in front of the camera and let their natural charisma do the rest. Plots were thin but the screen magic is undeniable.

The empress of underground movie drag was, undeniably, a tubby chap from Baltimore named Harris Glenn Milstead, aka Divine. With Divine, John Waters created a whole new genre. Divine was not a drag queen. As Waters explains in his autobiography *Shock Value*, 'Divine is simply an actor who is cast as a woman. A man playing women's roles'. The unique magic of the Waters *oeuvre* comes from the fact that Divine stomps and wiggles through these movies –

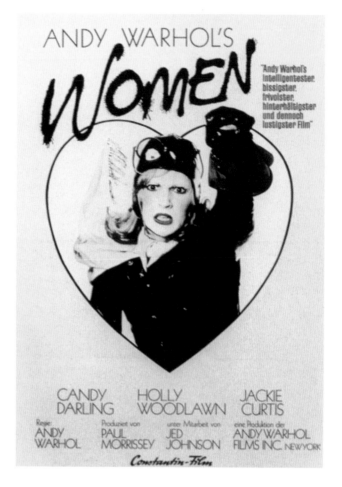

above
Candy Darling and Holly Woodlawn appeared every bit as glamorous as the movie queens of the day such as Faye Dunaway and Ali MacGraw. Jackie Curtis – he/she famously had boy periods and girl periods – was an enthusiastic proponent of the notion of gender fluidity.

opposite
After eating poodle poop off the sidewalk in *Pink Flamingos*, Divine becomes 'the filthiest person alive', and the most famous underground drag star of all time.

shopping, copulating, shooting people, cooking, stealing, having children – and is never acknowledged to be a man. This audacious piece of poetic licence is a strangely successful recipe for humour and satire. 'I'm still the top model in the country', proclaims the obese and scarred Divine in *Female Trouble*, forcing us to see the utter pointlessness of respecting conventional beauty standards. In many of Waters's movies – *Female Trouble*, *Polyester*, *Hairspray* – Divine loudly laments the burdens of womanhood. There is something deeply perverse about this conceit: an obvious man in a frock, kvetching about female problems in an *en passant* manner, daring the audience to question the premise.

The Rocky Horror Picture Show gave us the sweet transvestite from Transylvania, Dr. Frank-N-Furter, a cross-dressing predator who debunked the terror of *Psycho*, combining it with the preposterous hilarity of *Some Like It Hot*. As *Rocky Horror* became a global staple of midnight shows – Roger Ebert called it 'more of a long-running social phenomenon' – many hetero dudes felt permission to put on kinky lingerie and corsetry. The underground was now overground.

By the 1980s, drag – no longer so remote or threatening – was losing its power to communicate any kind of sinister agenda. Straight lads were wearing turquoise Lycra and bleaching their heavy-metal tresses. When they weren't listening to Def Leppard and Twisted Sister, they were donning black corsets and attending midnight screenings of *The Rocky Horror Picture Show* or *Pink Flamingos*. Drag became family-friendly. Kinky or sordid drag characters were not going to win Academy Awards during the Reagan years, the years when AIDS was ravaging the gay and trans communities. Movie drag became upbeat, non-sexual, non-homicidal, and worthy.

In 1982 Dustin Hoffman played a neurotic actor, who is driven to drag – he transforms himself into a beloved soap queen, Dorothy Michaels, aka Tootsie – in order to keep working. Through his covert transformation he gains insights into sexism and is forced to reflect upon his own previous temperamental ways. Thanks to *Tootsie*, dragging up is now equated not with madness and death, but with

below left
Julie Andrews not only avoids starvation but also gains personal insights by masquerading as a man who dresses as a woman in Blake Edwards's 1982 blockbuster *Victor Victoria*. The movie itself garnered seven Oscar nominations, while Andrews won a Golden Globe for her performance.

below right
In 1983 Barbra Streisand, the inspiration to so many drag queens, starred in *Yentl*, the story of a girl who cross-dresses in order to study Talmudic law. A subsequent movie titled *Nuts* is frequently referred to as 'Yentl goes Mental'.

consciousness-raising. One year later Barbra Streisand directs and stars in *Yentl*, an award-winning film about an earnest young lady who drags up in order to be permitted to study the Torah.

Drag movies snagged awards and became big business. The comfort level with drag was sufficiently high that directors moved on from making worthy movies about straight men who were forced to wear drag – learning life lessons in the process – and began to make movies *about* drag queens and trans people. A series of shrill drag-positive movies ensued, including *La Cage aux Folles*, *The Birdcage*, *The Adventures of Priscilla, Queen of the Desert*, and its

1993. Robin Williams plays a guy in the middle of an acrimonious divorce. He drags up as a nanny in order to gain access to his own children. Wearing drag is depicted as heroic and sacrificial. Any potential creepiness is expunged by Williams's brilliant slapstick moments. The 2007 *Guinness World Records* names *Mrs. Doubtfire* as the highest-grossing cross-dressing movie of all time.

The three drag queens in *The Adventures of Priscilla, Queen of the Desert* – Anthony (Hugo Weaving), Adam (Guy Pearce) and Bernadette (a trans woman played by Terence Stamp) – rampage across the Australian outback, spreading joy, unconventionality and sequins. All three actors were straight.

sequel, *To Wong Foo, Thanks for Everything, Julie Newmar*. Straight actors began to drag up as drag queens. In these films, a cartoony genre of drag and drag queenery is used to celebrate creativity, eccentricity and individuality, and to denounce old-fashioned or intolerant thinking.

Not every director in the 1980s and 1990s was painting with broad strokes: Sally Potter's *Orlando* is drenched in subtle poetic musings on gender and drag. This haunting movie depicts the life of an effeminate aristo who mysteriously changes sex and then lives for another 300 years. In *The Crying Game*, director Neil Jordan cast Jaye Davidson as Dil, the trans woman girlfriend of Jody, a soldier played by Forest Whitaker. This movie was praised for its subtlety and nuance, and for the creation of Dil, a sympathetic and intriguing character. The late revelation of Dil's trans status is a brilliant device that dares the mainstream audience to withdraw its approval and support. Even after the shock exposure of Dil's private parts, we are forced to treat this character as a regular human being and to empathize, and keep on empathizing.

Reigning queen of cinematic androgyny, Tilda Swinton serves Elizabethan drag in the 1992 film adaptation of Virginia Woolf's *Orlando*, a novel inspired by Woolf's gender-fluid pal Vita Sackville-West. An added drag bonus: Quentin Crisp, the self-described 'stately homo of England', frocks up as Queen Elizabeth I.

opposite
Jaye Davidson, a gay male, played Dil, a trans woman and the heart and the soul of Neil Jordan's *The Crying Game*, receiving an Academy Award nomination for Best Actor.

The late twentieth century saw the continuation of the bawdy, farcical side of drag with John Travolta's star turn as Edna Turnblad in the remake of John Waters's *Hairspray*, and most notably with Tyler Perry's massively successful Madea movies (see page 138). Running parallel to Perry were serious movies that humanized and romanticized drag and trans, most notably by Pedro Almodóvar.

Almodóvar's melodramatic films are filled with costumed transformation: nuns, bullfighters, etc. As Almodóvar-watcher June Thomas has noted: 'Given this obsession with exaggerated versions of womanhood and the rituals of dressing, as well as his roots in the underground and gay culture, it shouldn't be surprising that Almodóvar has used drag queens, transvestites, and transsexuals to explore questions of authenticity, ambition and romanticism.'

John Travolta, walking in very big shoes for the remake of *Hairspray*. In 2007 Travolta strapped on the falsies to play Edna Turnblad, the role originated with magnificent aplomb by the late great Divine in the original 1988 John Waters movie.

2004. Pedro Almodóvar's
Bad Education was the first
Spanish movie to open the
Cannes Film Festival. Gael
García Bernal plays Juan, then
Ángel Andrade, then Zahara,
a drag queen who is also a
transsexual.

Pedro Almodóvar is an Academy Award winner whose idiosyncratic movies, 19 to date, have had an enormous influence. His frequent use of trans and drag characters – *Law of Desire*, *High Heels*, *Bad Education* – have liberated other directors and steered the twenty-first-century cultural conversation through drag and towards trans. Thanks to Almodóvar, trans became Oscar bait. In 2005 Felicity Huffman won a Golden Globe for her depiction of a man becoming a woman in *Transamerica*. In 2013 Jared Leto dragged up to play a trans woman in *Dallas Buyers Club* and won a Best Actor Oscar. In 2015 Eddie Redmayne won an Oscar nod for his portrayal of an emerging trans woman in *The Danish Girl*. I use the term 'drag' in these instances because the actors themselves were not trans, and were therefore wearing drag in order to play trans. Dragging up to play trans has become the challenge every actor now longs for.

At last, trans actors get to play trans. *Tangerine* is a groundbreaking 2015 movie that combines the early Warhol approach – find charismatic gender-fluid individuals and let the cameras roll – with more solid plotlines. It is also very Warholian in that the individuals are not presented as noble or worthy. They just are. The trans women of *Tangerine* struggle at the bottom of society, causing mayhem, facing abuse and discrimination, but somehow exuding an enviable freedom.

In today's fragmenting media landscape, progressive movies like *Tangerine* are more likely to be found sliced up and made into a TV series. In contemporary culture, television, that former bastion of mainstream conventional tastes, has largely replaced movies as a platform for progressive ideas, making it a more welcoming place for drag and trans, as evidenced by the success of the series *Transparent*, *I Am Cait* and *Orange Is the New Black*. For those seeking unconventional queer narratives, binge-watching on your iPad has replaced schlepping to the movies.

Transformational roles win awards. Jared Leto received an Oscar gong for his portrayal of Rayon in *Dallas Buyers Club*.

Welcome to the future. *Tangerine* was shot on three iPhone 5s. The trans stars, Mya Taylor as Alexandra and Kitana Kiki Rodriguez as Sin-Dee Rella, were discovered at the Los Angeles LGBT Center and had little acting experience. This strangely touching movie garnered many awards, including a Best Actress Independent Spirit Award for Taylor.

CHAPTER 9

Radical Drag

I n 1870 a man named Ernest Boulton, a flamboyant gay whose drag name was Stella and who turned tricks to pay the rent, donned a cherry-coloured silk frock and headed off to London's Royal Strand Theatre. Here he cavorted openly with a frock-wearing male companion named Fanny. At some point Stella needed to pee, whereupon he skipped off to the ladies' loo, whereupon he was arrested on the charge of sodomy.

Stella was a reckless and fabulous character who broke every Victorian taboo and whose tabloid scandal riveted nineteenth-century Britain. The most sizzling revelations concerned Stella's masquerade as Lady Stella Pelham-Clinton, wife of Tory MP Lord Arthur Pelham-Clinton. Lord Arthur was subpoenaed to testify but committed suicide, allegedly, before submitting to this ordeal (his family claimed scarlet fever).

Marsha P. Johnson, activist, Stonewall frontliner, self-proclaimed drag queen and trans icon, was found floating in the Hudson River in 1992. The mystery of her death has yet to be solved.

'Hell hath no fury like a drag queen scorned.'

SYLVIA RIVERA in 1986, responding to an early draft of the New York Gay Rights Bill, which overlooked the transgender community

The uptight Victorian public could not believe that anyone, let alone a middle-class boy from Maida Vale, might possess the unmitigated gall to flounce about the West End of London in a frock, chirping lewd suggestions at passers-by. Stella's lawyer had no trouble persuading the naive jury that his client was merely a high-spirited youth with a taste for theatrical costume, *and he got off.* Stella fled to New York and became a successful female impersonator. At some point he returned to England and died in reduced circumstances, aged 56.

Stella's 'fuck you' to Victorian society lives on as a beacon of rebellion and a great example of the intrinsically subversive nature of drag. Even when done in jest, the donning of a frock or a drag king suit is a provocation that automatically messes with the stale conventions of any society.

Stella's saga took place well over a century and a half ago. Anti-cross-dressing laws persisted long after her death. New trends in dress during the twentieth century made it hard to prosecute offenders, but the intolerant laws remained on the books and were used as a flexible tool to harass masculine women and anyone identifying as transgender or gender non-conforming. As a result, drag, unless performed on a stage by an allegedly straight entertainer, remained in the shadows throughout the first half of the twentieth century.

Like followers of an oppressed religion, those who cross-dress have frequently been forced to worship in private. Casa Susanna was a transvestite retreat in the Catskills – a safe space long before the

Living la vida loca in Victorian England, c. 1871: Stella and Fanny, aka Thomas Ernest Boulton (right) and Frederick William Park.

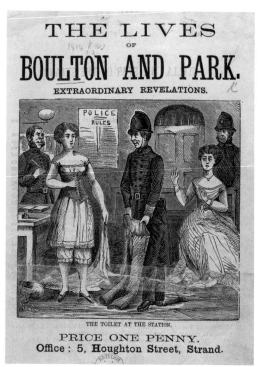

THE LIVES OF BOULTON AND PARK. EXTRAORDINARY REVELATIONS.

THE TOILET AT THE STATION.

PRICE ONE PENNY.
Office : 5, Houghton Street, Strand.

term was invented – run by Susanna Valenti and her wife, who conveniently ran the local wig store. Fifty years after this picture was taken, the secret documentation of Casa Susanna ended up in a Manhattan flea market. Robert Swope and Michel Hurst published the images into a book. Without this chance encounter, the radical and courageous secret of Casa Susanna might have been lost to history.

When, in the late 1960s, the counter-culture began to bloom – black power, gay lib, women's lib – drag followed suit. With the gays for solidarity, drag finally had the support it needed to hit the streets and to walk tall, sort of. Harassment and discrimination continued, but this time the dragsters fought back, birthing new and creative genres of drag activism. Three radical drag groups – the Cockettes, the Sisters of Perpetual Indulgence and the Radical Faeries – emerged from the political turmoil.

Snap time at Casa Susanna. Photography and transvestism are inextricably linked, and not always in a good way. Professional developers, if they were so inclined, might choose to call the police or even blackmail their customers, hence the popularity of Polaroids.

The personal is political: a courageous individual makes a powerful statement about gender identity at the 1975 New York City Gay Pride Day March (Gay Liberation Day). The improvised costume – and the bisected hair! – are both poignant and memorable.

The Cockettes

When one thinks of glitter-encrusted beards, one thinks of the Cockettes. In 1969 a guy named Hibiscus (George Edgerly Harris III) joined a flamboyant Haight-Ashbury commune named Kaliflower, and the Cockettes were born. Stage shows followed with names like *Tinsel Tarts in a Hot Coma* and *Journey to the Center of Uranus*. One of their most politically oriented productions was a short movie entitled *Tricia's Wedding*, a satire of the wedding of Richard Nixon's daughter. In 1971 the Cockettes, having gained national attention, were booked to perform in NYC. The shambolic, anti-rehearsed charm of their unstructured performance failed to impress the trendy New York elite. Andy Warhol and Angela Lansbury walked out. 'Having no talent is not enough', quipped Gore Vidal. The New Yorkers missed the point: it was messy because it was supposed to be messy.

The Cockettes pioneered a delightfully amateurish do-it-yourself genre of performance drag – the mouldy glam of Jack Smith writ large – that combined scavengings from thrift shops, home-made couture, crafty accessorizing and the trippy delights of glitter, tinsel and sequins. Vintage hats, ratty wigs, sloppily applied makeup and glittered beards completed the look. This 'assemblage' approach anticipated the wearable art movement.

The Cockettes' style was nothing if not gender-fluid. Boys dressed as girls. Girls dressed as boys dressed as girls. As former Cockette Fayette Hauser puts it, 'we wanted to fuck with people's idea of sex and gender along with any other category of human behaviour that required some solid unleashing. If anything, it was our politic to be as omni-gender as possible.'

The Sisters of
Perpetual Indulgence

Drag has been a symbol of decadence, moral decline and general ungodliness since Caligula threw on a handwoven hemp shift dress. Much of the intolerance directed at the LGBTQ world has been religiously motivated. Drag has been an easy target for those – Mary Whitehouse, Anita Bryant, Jerry Falwell and all those 'moral majority' leaders – who are looking for sinners to convert, or burn at the stake. How to combat religious zealots? There's only one way: beat them at their own game, but with humour. Enter the Sisters of Perpetual Indulgence.

The Sisters kicked off in 1979 with a bout of impromptu street theatre, a spontaneous creative response to the preachers who had begun to descend on the Castro in San Francisco, preaching hellfire and damnation. A group of gays donned Belgian nuns' habits and a smidgen of makeup, and confronted the proselytizers. Over time their drag evolved: riffs on the extreme styles of Catholic nuns' habits were augmented with Mardi Gras elements of heavy goth glam makeup, massive fake bosoms and junky costume jewellery. The high camp ecclesiastical fashion show in Fellini's *Roma* springs easily to mind. By combining elements of religious piety with rampant decadent artifice, they successfully satirize conventions of gender and morality.

The Sisters have proven to be more perpetual than anyone might have imagined. Orders are now found internationally, focusing their devotions on LGBTQ activism and fundraising. They are big proponents of the drag queen tradition of name puns: examples include Sister Rhoda Kill and Sister Stigmata Hari.

The Radical Faeries (overleaf)

Founded in the late 1970s in – you guessed it – California, the Radical Faeries embody many aspects of the counter-culture, including environmentalism, paganism, communal living and free love. Vigorously anti-establishment and anti-materialistic, they are a response to the increasing mainstreaming – mortgages! bank accounts! family life! ugh! – of gay culture. They nurture their outsider status by skipping through the woods and enjoying clothing-optional fairy gatherings.

With their drag, the Radical Faeries are so dégagé that they make the Cockettes look like an Oscar red carpet. Their drag is characterized by a wilful randomness and lack of rigour. Nudity and body paint are popular. When called upon to wear clothes, they might don hippyish shifts or granny's old peignoir. They accessorize with Birkenstocks and the occasional tambourine. Their drag is the key to their considerable charm, and very much in keeping with their 'everything is groovy' accepting ethos.

For Pride parades and special occasions, the Radical Faeries often make an effort to specifically resemble actual fairies, with floaty chiffon wings and sandals. I vividly recall, in the late 1980s, when they danced their way down Fifth Avenue during the annual Gay Pride parade wearing home-made diaphanous fairy frocks. Spectators cheered and then, when it became clear that the cartwheeling Faeries were not wearing foundation garments, rapidly averted their gazes. Once they reached Christopher Street they gathered together around a coffin containing a Judy Garland impersonator (*Oz* Judy is a Radical Faery icon). They banged their tambourines and chanted until Dorothy came back from the dead.

Stand up and be counted: the radical drag Hall of Fame

The scope and history of radical drag goes way beyond the Faeries, the Sisters and the Cockettes. Radical drag is also the story of highly idiosyncratic individual rebellion. Certain brave souls have, through a combination of daring, resilience and reckless disregard for their own safety, lubricated the wheels of social progress.

Stormé DeLarverie

Stormé DeLarverie's deep baritone and sartorial panache got her a job as a male impersonator – the only 'man'! – in the Jewel Box Revue (see page 23). Stormé (1920–2014) went on to become an icon of butch empowerment in Greenwich Village. Her bloody arrest by police at the Stonewall riots is said by many eyewitnesses to have been a pivotal moment.

> 'It was a rebellion, it was an uprising, it was a civil rights disobedience – it wasn't no damn riot.'

STORMÉ DELARVERIE, recalling Stonewall

Charlotte von Mahlsdorf

Charlotte von Mahlsdorf (1928–2002) witnessed the full brutality of history first-hand, living under one repressive regime after another. Sick of being abused by her Nazi father, she murdered him in his sleep, for which crime Teflon Charlotte only served four years in a reform school. One night she and a fellow transvestite (her preferred word) were arrested by the Hitler Youth, stripped and whipped. She narrowly avoided being sent to Sachsenhausen, the concentration camp where many gays and transvestites, wearing pink triangles, were tormented and exterminated alongside Jews. After the War many Holocaust-surviving gays and transfolk, contemporaries of Charlotte, were liberated, only to be immediately reimprisoned under German law for decades for the crime of homosexuality (and you thought your life sucked). The German government finally apologized for this astonishing cruelty in 2002.

After the War Charlotte lived under the Stasi in East Germany, miraculously surviving years of harassment, abuse and then far-right skinhead attacks, to see the Berlin Wall fall. Her endurance may in small part be due to her chosen mode of drag: she consciously eschewed the flamboyant decadent drag that one associates with the glamorous pre-War years of German cabaret, in favour of a more restrained hausfrau style. Her life was the subject of a magical documentary by (male) director Rosa von Praunheim.

José Julio Sarria

José Julio Sarria (1922–2013), shimmering
drag star of the Black Cat bar in San
Francisco, was known for integrating
political sloganeering into his drag act –
'There's nothing wrong with being gay – the
crime is getting caught' and 'United we
stand, divided they catch us one by one'
being a couple of fine examples. In 1961
this Second World War vet became the first
openly gay candidate to run for public office
in the USA. His drag was nothing if not regal:
he is remembered as the founder of the
Imperial Court System, a bejewelled drag
pageant fundraising organization that now
has chapters in over 68 US cities.

Radical Drag

Rollerena

Legendary New York nightclub Studio 54 was about celebrity, hedonism, materialism, high fashion and cocaine. Scything across the dance floor, through the preening and self-indulgent crowd, was a bespectacled roller-skating drag queen in a tatty wedding dress, carrying a fairy wand. Rollerena's haunting Havisham-esque presence added a much-needed element of bohemianism and performance art to the sea of Spandex jeans and Halston gowns. The power of Rollerena's gliding presence, night after night, came from her enigma: nobody quite knew what her deal was. Was she a Cockette? A Radical Faery? Some claimed that she was a Vietnam vet.

Joan Jett Blakk

Chicagoan Terence Smith, aka Joan Jett Blakk, did not believe in elaborate drag: a pair of cool shades, an Afro and a pair of fishnets, and Miss Jett Blakk was good to go. In 1991, encouraged by Queer Nation Chicago, Joan decided it was time for change and ran for mayor against Richard Daley. Her slogan? 'Fuck Dick Daley, with my dick daily.'

Undeterred by a loss, Joan followed this campaign with a run for the US presidency: 'My platforms, why tell you about them when you can see them for yourself? There they are, I walk on them every day. I'd like to see Bill [Clinton] wear these.' Joan used drag queen drollery to draw attention to the needs of the LGBTQ community while highlighting the race and class inequities of the political system.

Sylvia Rivera

Up there with Marsha P. Johnson, Sylvia Rivera (1951–2002) is one of the rad drag icons of history. Anti-assimilationist, she railed against the gay preoccupations with marriage equality and joining the military. She was focused on the neediest trans people, like herself, who were stuck at the bottom of society. In 1970 Sylvia and Marsha founded the Street Transvestite Action Revolutionaries (STAR), a group dedicated to helping homeless young drag queens and women of colour.

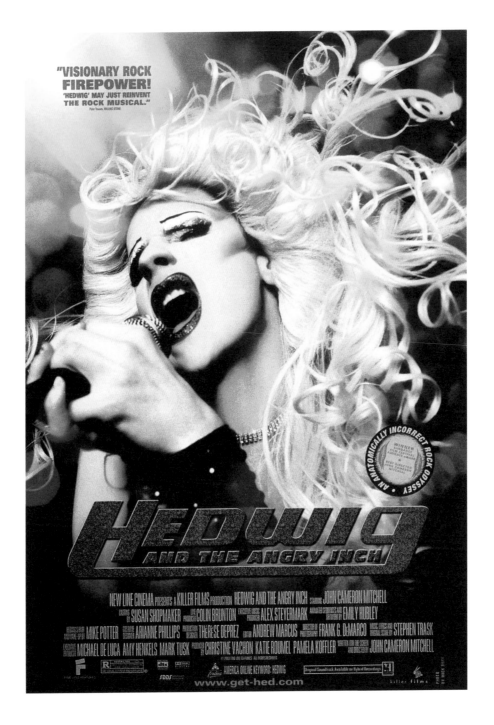

Hedwig

The most successful trans-themed musical of all time is *Hedwig and the Angry Inch*, a collaboration between John Cameron Mitchell and songwriter Stephen Trask that anticipated the gender revolution by a couple of decades. More serious and less camp than *The Rocky Horror Picture Show*, this tale of glam rock, paternal molestation, maternal neglect, botched gender reassignment surgery, love, betrayal and abandonment vibrates with radical political rage. Cameron Mitchell's strange and provocative creation – he played Hedwig in many productions and in the movie version – is a hard-rocking tour de force, which helped bring the trans conversation to a wider audience.

Panti Bliss

I was 15 years old when homosexuality was decriminalized in England. I was 41 years old when it was decriminalized in the Republic of Ireland, and 61 by the time same-sex marriage was legalized there. It takes guts and persistence to create change in a small religious country. Enter the face of Irish marriage equality, Panti Bliss, aka Rory O'Neill. Panti's biggest activist moment occurred on 11 January 2014, when she appeared on television channel RTE and called out journalists who she deemed to be homophobic. The named and shamed responded by suing RTE, which caved, allowing the litigants to walk away with many thousands of Euros. Panti responded by delivering an irrefutably rational speech at the famous Abbey Theatre in Dublin. Her oration, viewable on YouTube, instantly became a radical drag classic.

Buck Angel

'I don't need a penis to feel like a dude', says porn actor and entrepreneur Buck Angel. After an agonizing 28 years in the wrong body, Susan became Buck Angel, a manly man sans penis, a super-butch tattooed Tom of Finland archetype, with a vagina. Buck's radical redefining of penis-less masculinity – The Man With a Pussy – is a benchmark for radical trans/drag history.

Taylor Mac

Taylor Mac's preferred pronoun is 'judy' (lower case). Taylor's thought-provoking performances – judy has performed in highbrow venues including Lincoln Center and the Sydney Opera House – won judy an astonishing number of awards including a MacArthur Foundation Genius Grant. Taylor's ability to penetrate the high-culture establishment with judy's brave and crazy *oeuvre* – one performance requires Mac to sing 246 songs in 24 straight hours – makes judy a powerfully radical drag queen.

Radical drag gets the Trump bump

It looked for a moment as if drag would chug happily into the future on a raft of creative gender exploration, performance art and elaborately painted look queens like Ryan Burke (see page 233). Then Trump happened, and glamour drag, comedy drag and their wild untamable sister, radical drag, each received their call-up papers.

After the 2016 US election result, drag queen Marti G. Cummings did some digging. When Marti found out that her very own neighbourhood Democratic Club had been shamefully inactive throughout the run-up to the election, she took charge of it herself. She was one of many drag queens who woke up after the election and reached for the eyelash glue. Lady Bunny released a Trump White House-themed satire of ''Twas the Night Before Christmas'. Rad drag comedians and transfolk like Merrie Cherry, Sarah Maywalt, Charlene and Ruby Roo all began to let rip. 'It was out of anger when I started [doing drag]', *Drag Race* star Alaska told DragCon attendees in 2017, adding, 'and when Trump was put into office, that anger was reignited.' Radical drag seeped into the entire drag spectrum.

British-Iraqi writer, drag performer and filmmaker Amrou Al-Kadhi first gained notoriety as part of a beloved UK drag troupe named Denim. Their work – gender-fluid Amrou goes by 'they' – explores the politics of queer identity, cultural representation and race. A Cambridge grad with no shortage of radical ideas, Amrou/Glamrou claims that 'Quantum physics really helped me understand my queer identity'.

Three-time Oscar winner, and now proud drag king, Meryl Streep paid homage to the 45th President of the United States at the 2016 Public Theater Gala.

But what makes drag so wickedly compelling in these new politicized times? According to drag queen Gilda Wabbit, drag ensures that any political message hits home, 'like a strong drink before a tough conversation'. And then there is that Medusa effect. Speaking to *The New York Times*, Alabama activist Ambrosia Starling underscored the mesmerizing visual power of a fierce diva drag queen on any crowd: 'Who's going to pay attention to a 40-year-old queer standing on the steps with a bunch of queers? I wanted those cameras to look and not look away.'

Does this new movement have a leader? Late-night talk show host John Oliver thinks so. He suggested that RuPaul could run for president using the slogan 'Make America Fierce Again'. RuPaul's first post-Trump DragCon event offered political panels with drag stars such as Bob the Drag Queen. Ru declared, 'I understand what it is we must do. We're going to mobilize young people who have never been mobilized, through our love of music, our love of love, our love of bright colours.' Ads for *RuPaul's Drag Race* season 9 featured the tagline 'Drastic times call for dragtastic measures', and RuPaul's own Twitter feed began to sparkle with unflattering allusions to the 'Manchurian pumpkin'. 'I'm not doing drag to give you makeup tips', RuPaul declared, adding, 'This has always been a political statement.'

Some have suggested that Trump, with his makeup, wig, penchant for drama and exaggerated gestures, verges on being a drag queen himself. Speaking to *The New York Times*, RuPaul pooh-poohed this theory: 'As drag queens, we know we're putting on a facade and we're always aware of it, which is what scares the status quo. He believes he looks good. He believes he's looking like a real man.' He is, in other words, perfect drag king fodder for any and all of those brilliant butches who satirize toxic masculinity with such panache.

And the subversive dragtastic drag kings of the world are on *fuego*. Kristine BellaLuna (aka Landon Cider), Kandee Johnson, Kat Sketch – to name but three – are creating Insta vids and YouTube tutorials in which they drag-kingify themselves into The Donald. Technology and social media are disseminating mocking, shocking, radical, satirical drag far and wide into every corner of the universe. Is it gonna be yuuuge? It already is.

More than a look queen: Ryan Burke's exquisite self-portraits propel the whole concept of look queening into the realm of radical psychedelia.

The Library is Open

Mark Francis, Margery King and Hilton Als, *The Warhol Look: Glamour, Style, Fashion*, Bulfinch Press, 1997

Philip Core, *Camp: The Lie That Tells the Truth*, Plexus Publishing, 1984

Judith 'Jack' Halberstam and Del LaGrace Volcano, *The Drag King Book*, Serpent's Tail, 1999

Bianca Del Rio, *Blame it on Bianca Del Rio*, Dey Street Books, 2018

Sue Tilley, *Leigh Bowery: The Life and Times of an Icon*, Hodder and Stoughton, 1997

Grayson Perry and Wendy Jones, *Grayson Perry: Portrait of the Artist as a Young Girl*, Vintage, 2006

Camille Paglia, *Sexual Personae: Art and Decadence from Nefertiti to Emily Dickinson*, Yale University Press, 1990

Camille Paglia, *Vamps & Tramps: New Essays*, Vintage, 1994

Amanda Lear, *My Life with Dalí*, Virgin Books, 1985

Kris Kirk and Ed Heath, *Men in Frocks*, Gay Men's Press, 1984

Marjorie Garber, *Vested Interests: Cross-Dressing and Cultural Anxiety*, Routledge, 2012

Charlotte von Mahlsdorf, *I Am My Own Wife: The True Story of Charlotte von Mahlsdorf*, Cleis Press, 2004

Martin Aston, *Breaking Down the Walls of Heartache: How Music Came Out*, Constable, 2016

Julian Fleisher, *The Drag Queens of New York: An Illustrated Field Guide*, Riverhead Books, 1996

Candy Darling, intr. Jeremiah Newton, *My Face for the World to See: The Diaries, Letters, and Drawings of Candy Darling, Andy Warhol Superstar*, Hardy Marks Publications, 1997

Alison Lurie, *The Language of Clothes*, Vintage, 1983

Holly Brubach, *Girlfriend: Men, Women, and Drag*, Random House, 1999

Roger Baker, *Drag: A History of Female Impersonation in the Performing Arts*, New York University Press, 1994

Holly Woodlawn with Jeff Copeland, *A Low Life in High Heels: The Holly Woodlawn Story*, St Martin's Press, 1991

Index

Picture Credits

Every effort has been made to contact the copyright holders of the illustrations, but should there be any errors or omissions, the publisher would be pleased to insert the appropriate acknowledgement in any subsequent printing of this book.

FRONT COVER: © Albert Sanchez
BACK COVER: Simon Fowler / LFI / Avalon

2 Everett Collection Inc / Alamy Stock Photo **6** © Albert Sanchez **8** © Vincent Sandoval / Getty Images **9** © Santiago Felipe / FilmMagic / Getty Images **10** © David Belisle **11** © Erik McGregor / Pacific Press / LightRocket via Getty Images **12** © Albert Sanchez **14** © Santiago Felipe/ Getty Images **15** © Rodin Eckenroth/ WireImage/Getty Images **16** Author's own collection **17** © Angela Weiss/AFP/Getty Images **19** © Matthew Kiernan / Alamy Stock Photo **20** Image courtesy of Norman Von Holtzendorff **21** © Arthur Benda/ ullstein bild via Getty Images **22** Author's own collection **23** © David Wharry/BIPs/ Getty Images **25** Photo by Movie Poster Image Art/Getty Images **27** Photo by Keystone-France / Gamma-Keystone via Getty Images **29** © Martin Godwin/Getty Images **30** Everett Collection Inc / Alamy Stock Photo **31 (top l)** Lane Turner/The Boston Globe via Getty Images **31 (top r)** © Nick Rogers/ANL/REX/Shutterstock **31 (bottom r)** austin@austinyoung.com **32** J.M. Fonteneau **33** Everett Collection, Inc. / Alamy Stock Photo **34 (top)** © Patrick McMullan via Getty Images **34 (bottom)** © David Yarritu **35** © Linda Simpson **36** Daniel SIMON / Gamma-Rapho via Getty Images **37** © Albert Sanchez **39 (r)** Courtesy Todd Oldham **41** © Roxanne Lowit **42** © Albert Sanchez **43** © Santiago Felipe/Getty Images **44** © Lisa Maree Williams / Getty Images **46** © Association Marcel Duchamp / ADAGP, Paris and DACS, London   Photo Heritage Image Partnership Ltd / Alamy Stock Photo **47** © Succession Marcel Duchamp/ ADAGP, Paris and DACS, London / © Man Ray Trust/ADAGP, Paris and DACS, London **48** © Jersey Heritage Trust **49** © 2019 The Andy Warhol Foundation for the Visual Arts, Inc. / Licensed by DACS, London. Photo ©Scala, Florence/BPK, Bildagentur fuer Kunst, Kultur und Geschichte, Berlin **50** Copyright Jack Smith Archive Courtesy Gladstone Gallery, New York and Brussels **51** © 2019 The Andy Warhol Foundation for the Visual Arts, Inc. / Licensed by DACS, London. Photo © Christies/Bridgeman **52** © Graham Smith/PYMCA/REX/Shutterstock **53** Courtesy Time Out **55** © David Swindells/PYMCA/Avalon **56** © ARNO BURGI / AFP / Getty Images **57** © Becker & Bredel/ullstein bild via Getty Images **58** © CHRISTER STRÖMHOLM / STRÖMHOLM ESTATE **59** © Henny Garfunkel **60** © David LaChapelle **61** © Holly Falconer **62** © Zachary Krevitt and Thomas McCarty / NYT / Redux / eyevine **63** © Cameron Cuchulainn 2017 **64** © Jack Taylor/Getty Images **66** © Holly Falconer **67** News Dog Media **68** Fox Photos/Getty Images **69 (l)** © George Platt Lynes **69 (r)** © E.O. Hoppé Estate Collection / Curatorial Assistance Inc. **70** © Lucien Samaha, www.luciensamaha. net **71** Courtesy Bridgeman Images **72** © Paul Thompson / FPG / Getty Images **73** SNAP / REX / Shutterstock **74** Bettmann/ Getty Images **75 (l)** Pictorial Press Ltd / Alamy Stock Photo **75 (r)** Syndication International/Getty Images **77** Collection of the Smithsonian National Museum of African American History and Culture **78** The History Collection / Alamy Stock Photo **79** Atomic / Alamy Stock Photo **80** Margaret Chute/Hulton Archive/Getty Images **81** Hulton Archive/Getty Images **82** © Albert Sanchez **83** Bennett Raglin/ BET/Getty Images for BET **84** © Albert Sanchez **86** Fred W. McDarrah/Getty Images **87** © Albert Sanchez **88** Courtesy Numero Group **89** Everett Collection/ Mary Evans Picture Library **91 (r)** © Brian Lantelme **93** Courtesy of CHEAP **95** Santiago Felipe/Getty Images for RuPaul's Drag Race **96** Noam Galai/WireImage/ Getty Images **97** Rodin Eckenroth/Wire-Image/Getty images **98** Jeff Kravitz/ FilmMagic/Getty Images **100** Thomas Niedermueller / Life Ball 2013 / Getty Images **101** © Krisanne Johnson **102** Dimitrios Kambouris / WireImage / Getty Images **104** Art Collection 3 / Alamy Stock Photo **105** Shutterstock **106** Shutterstock **107** © Quattrone, Florence **108** Painters /

LAURENCE KING

Published in 2019 by
Laurence King Publishing Ltd
361–373 City Road
London EC1V 1LR
United Kingdom
email: enquiries@laurenceking.com
www.laurenceking.com

A catalogue record for this book
is available from the British Library

ISBN: 978-1-78627-423-6

Picture Research: Heather Vickers
Senior Editor: Felicity Maunder
Design: Alexandre Coco

Printed in China

Laurence King Publishing is committed to
ethical and sustainable production. We are
proud participants in The Book Chain Project ®
Bookchainproject.com

Author's acknowledgements

Special thanks to Albert Sanchez and Pedro Zalba,
whose glorious photographs elevate the art of drag

Norman Von Holtzendorff

Natalie Andrews

Vaginal Davis

Professor Amy Adler

Billy Erb/Billy Beyond

Will Higdon-Sudow

Aaron Sciandra and Garry Hannon

Mark Vitulano

Aida Yohannes

Mo B. Dick

Felicity Maunder

Heather Vickers

Alex Coco

Camilla Morton

Author and drag enthusiast, **Simon Doonan** is
the Creative Ambassador for Barneys New York.
A longstanding member of the fashion community,
he is a regular guest on radio, TV and web, and a
judge on the NBC series *Making It*.

Front cover:
Violet Chachki, photographed
by Albert Sanchez

Back cover:
Freddie Mercury in
the video for Queen's
'I Want to Break Free'

Frontispiece:
Charles Pierce as Bette Davis